Giving GOD the GLORY

Keswick Ministry

Eric Alexander, Michael Baughen,
Philip Hacking, Stephen Olford,
Donald Bridge and others

Edited by
David Porter

STL Books
PO BOX 48, Bromley, Kent, England.
PO BOX 28, Waynesboro, Georgia, USA.
PO BOX 656, Bombay 1, India.

Keswick Convention Council, England.

Copyright © 1985 The Keswick Convention Council

STL Books are published by Send The Light (Operation Mobilisation),
PO Box 48, Bromley, Kent, England.

British Library Cataloguing in Publication Data

Giving God the glory : Keswick ministry : annual collection of Keswick
 convention sermons.
 1. Theology, Doctrinal
 I. Porter, David, *1945-*
 230   BT77.3

ISBN 1 85078 006 4

Typesetting and page make-up by Creative Editors & Writers Ltd,
Northwood, Middx.

Covers printed by Penderel Press Ltd, Croydon, Surrey.

Made and printed in Great Britain by Hunt Barnard Printing Ltd,
Aylesbury, Bucks.

CONTENTS

INTRODUCTION

by Rev Philip Hacking
(Chairman of the Keswick Convention Council)

You hold in your hands the essence of the ministry of the 1985 Keswick Convention; it includes both sets of Bible readings, and at least one address by each of the main speakers.

But a Convention is not only a series of addresses; it is a gathering of people in a particular place – in this case, the well-loved tents which stand in the lovely town of Keswick among the hills of the English Lakeland.

If you were one of those people who gathered in those tents this summer, you will have seen a number of changes. I do hope that you found them exciting and not at all unnerving! For example, we introduced a rather more flex-ible progamme in the evening, and took the opportunity to include songs, interviews, and chorus singing. These are the sort of things that young people in particular enjoy, but I think it's also true that a time of worshipping God together and having fellowship in this way prepares us all for the teaching that follows.

Of course we're not trying to diminish by one iota Kes-wick's emphasis on the Word of God. That would be fatal. What Keswick stands for is exposition, and if that goes –

we've had it! But our aim is to help people relax in worship.

We'd like to see a lot more young people at Keswick. Of course, we want the older folk to keep on coming! Many young people have come to faith in Jesus Christ recently, through Mission England, for example, but also through many other agencies. That's wonderful! And I believe that what we have to get across to them is that the Christian life needs to be solidly based on God's Word; so the ministry at Keswick has a particular relevance to younger people. And I've noticed that more and more of the young people have a real desire to study the Bible.

Having said that, one must say also that making them sit in one place for long periods of listening might not be the best way to encourage that interest – either in young people or in those of us who are older! So that is why we are introducing various elements into the evening sessions. We hope that it will add a certain liveliness which they – and all of us – will enjoy.

Another change is a long-term one. During the 1985 Convention we announced the beginning of our programme of building and renovation of the Skiddaw Street site. This will result in greatly improved facilities during the Convention and a much more comfortable environment for Convention meetings.

We are excited by this project, in which we have already seen God's hand and His encouragement. If you would like to be involved as a prayer-supporter or in any other way, write to the Secretary, Keswick Convention Council, 25 Camden Road, London NW1 9LN. We will be delighted to send you further details.

EDITOR'S INTRODUCTION

This was a year of change at Keswick, and there is more to come – during the Convention the building appeal was announced, which will greatly improve the site and ease the work of the organisers in future years. A new hymnbook sat side by side with the well-loved Keswick hymnbook on the seats this year, and both were well-used; and there were other changes, all of which seemed to be accepted with great good-humour by Conventioners.

Some things don't change, however. The weather was as variable as ever, and many of the speakers had to compete with driving rain on the canvas above them. For the few days that I was able to attend the Convention, it kept reasonably dry on the hills when I was walking and poured while I was sitting safely in the tent. There's probably a lesson somewhere in that.

Something else which changes very little is the pleasant task of editing the annual Keswick report each year.

The work owes a great deal to the army of volunteers who prepare the transcripts from which the final editing is done. In addition, the speakers graciously waive their right to check their material before it is printed, in order to make it possible to produce the book in time for Christmas. The Keswick Council liaises closely with the publishers, but it is important that the readers are aware that the book remains a record of spoken addresses given at a particular Convention.

The Rev Eric Alexander's Bible Readings in this year's volume, however, represent a slight departure from our usual methods, in that Mr Alexander provided us with his own comprehensive notes from which he gave the four Readings. We have added some of his asides and amplifications from the platform, to give the flavour of the event. The rest of the material in the volume has been edited to enable as wide a selection of the addresses as possible to be included.

The editorial policy has been to retain as much of the speaker's content as possible, and to include only some of the asides, illustrations, anecdotes and introductory material as is necessary to convey the flavour of the occasion. This means that a wealth of wit, humour and application has been omitted, and for this you must make use of the excellent tape library facilities mentioned elsewhere in the book.

We recommend that you read with a Bible beside you. Many Bible quotations have been abridged where this can be done without losing their relevance. Some which were given in full by the speakers are represented here only by their references. Where appropriate, biblical quotations have been checked against the text, but many speakers paraphrased to make a point; we have left such paraphrases unchanged.

Finally, thanks are due to my wife Tricia, who spent many hours typing the manuscript – time taken from a busy summer.

David Porter

THE BIBLE READINGS

GIVING GOD THE GLORY
(1 CORINTHIANS 1—4)

by Rev Eric Alexander

1. The Church of God
(1:1–17)

I turn to these chapters with you, because they deal with
certain foundation principles which the church of Jesus
Christ needs urgently to relearn in our generation. If one
were to try to identify the main thrust of this section of 1
Corinthians, it would be in terms of a summons to put God
rather than man at the centre of our thinking, in every
sphere of life: in our thinking about the church, about the
gospel, about the world, about the service of God, and
about the life of the man of God.

There is no doubt that most of the problems in the church
at Corinth arose from failure at precisely this point. There
was a pervasive man-centredness in the church; so they
gloried in man rather than in God, they boasted in human
achievements and distinctions and gifts rather than divine
accomplishment. They experienced factions and jealousies
and divisions in the church, and that led to distortions in
their view of the gospel, difficulties in relationships, and
carelessness about God's standards. And all these derived
from that fundamental sickness, a man-centredness in their
thinking.

So Paul takes up the words of Jeremiah 9:24, at the end

of 1 Corinthians 1: 'Let him who boasts boast in the Lord' (1:31). In one way or another, these four chapters are an exposition of that text and its implications. If you want to know the text for all that we shall be discovering in these four studies, it will be this.

And quite simply I want to say to you, that it is an increasing conviction on my own spirit that there is no emphasis we need more than this in the contemporary Christian church.

As you will know, Paul had come to Corinth in the course of his second missionary journey. He came with quite a catalogue of discouragements behind him. He had gone through that remarkable experience at Troas of being called to Macedonia; before that, he had experienced so many mysterious frustrations, as God seemed to be closing doors wherever they tried to go in Asia and Bithynia. You can read the story in Acts 16. Then there was this dramatic opening of a way to Greece, and you can imagine him saying: 'Ah, well; all the tribulations and frustrations were worthwhile.'

But the account of his ministry in Greece makes sober reading. In Philippi his visit was cut short by a prison sentence. In Thessalonica his ministry led to a riot, which pursued him to Berea. Led out of the troubles to Athens, Paul was met there by a mixture of amused tolerance, mockery and cynicism.

So it is not really surprising that he came to Corinth 'in weakness, fear, and much trembling'. And it was there that God taught him in a very special way a jealous zeal to exalt and boast in God rather than man.

Let us turn to the first seventeen verses of chapter 1, and we shall see how Paul applies these experiences to the theme of 'the church of God'. Verse 2 gives us the phrase, in Paul's address 'to the church of God in Corinth'. And in these verses, the apostle speaks to us about such themes as the church's foundation, origin, constitution, character, destiny and unity.

The foundation of the church

By this, I mean the foundation on which the church is built. That is what Paul is emphasising as he introduces himself in chapter 1, verse 1, in the way he commonly introduced his epistles. It is true to say that he is the *founder* of the church at Corinth (as Acts 18 makes clear), but to Paul, the more important truth is that as an apostle he is the *foundation* of the church. Ephesians 2:20 is one of the classic statements of this. The household of God is 'built on the foundation of the apostles and prophets'.

Let me clarify this a little, for it is of great importance today. The idea of apostleship has three applications in the New Testament. It has a simple and universal use for a messenger, or one who is sent for another, as in John 13:16. Secondly, it has a more specific use for those sent by the churches (2 Corinthians 8:23, where the word translated in the NIV as 'representatives' really means 'apostles').

But the third is the classic use of the word, applied to that select band to whom Jesus gave the title 'apostle' in Luke 6:13. In the New Testament the word is basically reserved for them and for Paul. They are appointed and commissioned by the Lord Jesus to teach with authority. That is the sense in which Paul says, in Ephesians 2:20, that God's church is built on the foundation of the apostles and prophets.

Let me say again, this is not the *persons* of the apostles. Paul specifically clarifies that in 1 Corinthians 3:11, when he says that the personal foundation of the church is Jesus Christ: 'No other foundation can any man lay than that which is laid which is Jesus Christ.' But the *doctrinal foundation* is apostolic teaching; and for us, that means holy Scripture.

You see, the Holy Spirit inspires the apostles and ourselves in different ways. He inspired the apostles to write scripture. He inspires us to understand, expound, believe and obey it.

Now that means that when we depart from apostolic doctrine, either by subtracting from or adding to it, we are eroding the very foundation of the church of God, grieving the Holy Spirit who inspired the apostles, dishonouring the Lord Jesus Christ who authorised them, and endangering the souls of God's people who need that apostolic authority for their wellbeing. It was a major mark of the sickness of the church at Corinth, that they questioned apostolic authority. So in 1 Corinthians 9:1 Paul has to ask, 'Am I not an apostle? Have I not seen Jesus our Lord?'

So the foundation of the church of God is apostolic doctrine. Let me now turn with you to the second theme of these verses:

The origin of the church

Quite simply, in verse 2, the origin of the church is in God. It is God's church, the creation of it was His plan, the calling of it is at His initiative, the ownership of it is in God's hands; it is the church of God which He obtained with the blood of His own Son (Acts 20:28).

So the origin of the church lies in God's activity, not ours. To that Jesus bears witness when He says 'I will build my church.'

More specifically in verse 4, the origin of the church lies in God's *grace*. This is what Paul chiefly thanks God for. The only thing which could have produced the church of

God in the city of Corinth was the grace of God in Jesus Christ.

That is more than just a doctrinal truth. Grace in the New Testament always has the distinctive sense of unmerited and unrepayable kindness to undeserving sinners. It is the only ground on which God deals with men. The method of grace is therefore the first lesson that sinners need to learn if they would experience the salvation of God.

But it is the continuing lesson that the church of Christ needs to learn if it would enjoy the blessing of God, and for this reason: it is the doctrine of pure grace which makes men boast in God, and prevents them from boasting in men.

So Paul says in Ephesians 2:8 'It is by grace you have been saved . . . not by works, lest any man should boast.' So in Romans 3, when he reaches the apex of his argument for justification by grace through faith, he asks, 'Where then is boasting?' (verse 27), and answers, 'It is excluded.'

Now that is something about which we need to be absolutely clear. From beginning to end, from our election in eternity to our glorification in heaven, salvation is God's work not man's, and all the glory for it belongs solely to Him. Grace and human boasting cannot co-exist. We need to learn that the only thing we contribute to our own salvation is the sin which makes it necessary, and that is why we have nothing in which to boast.

The constitution of the church

In verse 2, Paul describes and defines the constitution of the church. First, *the church of God in Corinth consists of those who are 'sanctified in Christ Jesus'*. That is a very significant phrase, and we need to unpack it a little. We normally think of sanctification as that life-long process in the believer by which we are changed into the image of Christ; that is, it is a change in character or condition. But here in 1 Corinthians 1:2 the verb is a perfect passive participle – that is, it refers to something already done in us and completed. The same usage is found in 1 Corinthians 6:11, where Paul tells the Corinthians 'You were washed, you were sanctified, you were justified in the name of the Lord Jesus Christ'.

In this usage, sanctification appears to precede justification, rather than follow it. The key to it is in the other half of the phrase 'in Christ Jesus' (which is a shorthand way of speaking of the believer's union with Christ).

When we become Christians, we are united to the Lord Jesus Christ (we 'believe into' the Lord Jesus Christ, and the Holy Spirit unites us to Him like branches to a vine or limbs to a body). Thus we are separated from the old life and the old regime of sin, and set apart for Christ.

Second, *the church consists of those who have been called by God and call upon Him*. Indeed, the very word *ekklesia* in verse 2 means 'the called ones' – those who have known the name of God. In fact, that is one of the New Testament's favourite ways of describing the Christian; called out of darkness into light, called into fellowship with His Son, called to be free, called to be holy, called with a heavenly calling.

Now the significant thing about this call is that it is not merely vocal and verbal. It is the sort of call which is illustrated in the raising of Lazarus, where Jesus called Lazarus out of darkness into light. Now there is nothing more pointless than calling to a dead man in a tomb – except when God is doing it, for then the authority of the voice carries the power to waken the dead and draw him from the grave. So Lazarus the dead man heard the voice of God and was brought from death to life by the call of God. Precisely this, in spiritual terms, is true of every Christian.

So the church of God consists of those who are called: called to be holy, called into fellowship with His Son Jesus Christ our Lord (verses 2 and 9).

But the second half of verse 2 tells us that the church also consists of all those everywhere who call upon the name of our Lord Jesus Christ. That is, the evidence that God has truly called us to Himself is that we call on Him, discovering as we do that whosoever calls on the name of the Lord shall be saved.

The Christian church, then, consists of those who are sanctified in Christ Jesus, who have been called to Himself by God, and who in turn join with all other believers in calling on the name of the Lord Jesus Christ. And that worldwide Christian community is united by a common submission to the lordship of Jesus. Note these significant words at the very end of verse 2: 'their Lord and ours'. That is what makes the church a worshipping, serving community.

The character of the church

From verse 4 Paul turns to thanksgiving; and in doing so, he describes some of the characteristics of the church of God.

First, *it is the product of grace*. Verse 4 tells us that every cause of thankfulness in the church is the product of God's grace. And that free unmerited mercy of God is encapsulated in all that Jesus Christ is to the believer. 'In Him you have been enriched in every way' (verse 5). The first evidence of that was that the apostles' preaching was confirmed or validated by the work of the Holy Spirit in bringing them to repentance and faith (verse 6).

So they who were without God, without Christ, and without hope (which is true poverty) are now possessors of all the riches of God in Christ Jesus. Paul just cites two ways in which they are enriched (verse 5): speech and knowledge. Their speech would be their own testimony to the grace of God, and their knowledge would in the ultimate sense be not just knowledge of the truth but knowledge of God.

That is the real enrichment grace brings us, that we may know God. That indeed is what Jeremiah 9:23 (which is Paul's 'text' in this section) speaks about: 'Let not the rich man boast of his riches. But let him who boasts boast in this, that he understands and knows me that I am the Lord.'

The faculty of knowledge is given to us so that we may know God, and the faculty of speech so that we may boast in Him.

The church of Jesus Christ should therefore above all be characterised as: 'The people who know their God.' That is what men and women ought to say of us. 'These are people who know God, and who make Him known.'

Second, *it is the possessor of gifts*. The words for 'grace' and 'gifts' are closely related in Greek. One is *charis*, the other is *charismata*. It is a work of God's grace that He gives gifts, spiritual gifts, to His church. In verse 7 Paul tells the Corinthians that they do not lack any spiritual gift. Clearly that is not addressed to an individual, but to the entire church.

There are three lists of these gifts in the New Testament: one in Romans 12, one in Ephesians 4, and one in 1 Corinthians 12. It is fairly certain that these lists are by no means exhaustive, and the gifts themselves are exceedingly diverse. They range from gifts of helps and administration and serving, to gifts of tongues and prophecy. Every believer is given some gift, so that the whole church does not lack any gift. The one thing that the possession of a gift must never make us is arrogant and proud, because all *charismata* derive from *charis*, all gifts derive from grace, and all are designed – exclusively designed – for God's glory.

That's why it worries me when people are more interested in the sensational, spectacular gifts which tend to draw attention to themselves, than they are in the self-effacing gifts, which are scarcely capable of glorifying self.

Third, *it is the preparation for glory* (verses 7 and 8). In one sense this is the great distinctive characteristic of the people of God. They live as those who wait eagerly for the revelation of the Lord Jesus Christ. Their eyes are upon Him, their hearts are indeed in another world. So in Philippians 3:20 Paul tells us that our citizenship is in heaven, from whence we look for our Lord Jesus.

Thus the church of Christ is like a colony of heaven on earth. We live as aliens on this earth, belonging and yet not belonging, living by different standards, judging by different criteria, owning allegiance to another King, marching to the beat of a different drummer. We are a colony of heaven; eagerly waiting for the arrival of our King, our chief ambition to be blameless on the day of His coming.

Is that a picture of the church of Christ in our contemporary experience? It is what our forefathers called 'heavenly-mindedness'. The sad thing is that we think we are rather clever today, when we despise and dismiss, with phrases like, 'He's so heavenly-minded he's no earthly use.' My dear friends, that is not the problem from which the modern world suffers. Our problem is precisely the reverse. But God intends us to be a people who are preparing for glory, and who experience some foretaste of it as we worship together in this world.

And that leads me to the fifth way in which Paul speaks to us of the church, in verses 8 and 9.

The destiny of the church

'He will sustain you to the end' (verse 8). That is the future hope of the church of Jesus Christ, and it is grounded on the persevering faithfulness of God who, having begun a good work in us, will go on to perfect it until the day of Christ. This hope is an absolute confidence that at the coming of Christ we shall be found in the same state of grace and acceptance as that in which we stand as Christians today. That is what 'blameless', or 'guiltless', in verse 8 refers to.

Notice in verse 9 that God's persevering faithfulness is illustrated in His calling us into fellowship with His Son Jesus Christ our Lord. Now in Romans 11:29 Paul tells us that 'God's gifts and his call are irrevocable'. So we are finally assured that on the day of Christ we shall be unimpeachable, because the call of Christ is irrevocable. 'He is faithful' – even, says Paul in 2 Timothy 2:13, if we are faithless.

That's persevering grace, my brothers and sisters! And what it means is that when the Lord Jesus hands over the kingdom to His Father, He will say 'Here am I, and the children you have given me . . . not one of them is lost' (*cf.* John 17).

Some years ago one of the national newspapers ran an article entitled, 'Is there a future for the church?' And of course the right answer is, 'It depends what you mean.' If by 'the church' you mean a particular denomination or organisation, the answer is 'not necessarily', because God nowhere promises to perpetuate any particular denomination or group.

But if you mean the church of Jesus Christ which is the people of God and the Body of Christ and the Temple of the Holy Spirit, the answer is that there is nothing in the future so secure. Everything that God is doing in the world focuses on the church of Christ which He is building. The rest of history is just the scaffolding behind which God is building His church. And one day He will dismantle that scaffolding, and there will be revealed the perfected church of His Son. God will say, 'Look at that! That's my master-piece!' And then, when the church is completed, He will bring down the curtain on history and pronounce it at an end. Oh, the beautiful construction, of His redeemed humanity!

That's the destiny of the church.

Lord Reith, that great Scotsman who was the first Direc-tor-General of the BBC, once went to visit a group of young avant-garde intellectuals who were preparing a pro-gramme. He asked them, 'What is the purpose of the pro-gramme?' And they said, 'It has the general theme of "Giv-ing the Christian church a decent burial."' And Reith, who was a great Christian, looked over his craggy eyebrows and stood up to his six feet and said to the spokesman, 'Young man; the church of Jesus Christ will stand at the grave of the BBC.' And so it will; and at the grave of every other merely human institution.

So we have the foundation of the church, the origin of the church, the character of the church, and the destiny of the church. In these closing moments, let me point out to you what Paul teaches us, in the rest of the passage from verse 10 to verse 17:

The unity of the church

He now turns from thanksgiving and assurance to exhorta-tion, and his appeal throughout verses 10 to 17 is an appeal for *unity*. Verse 10: 'I appeal to you, brothers, in the name of our Lord Jesus Christ, that all of you agree with one another so that there may be no divisions among you and that you may be perfectly united in mind and thought.'

Now, we need to distinguish from each other several words in the 'unity' family; such as 'unity', and 'union', and 'uniformity', and 'unanimity'.

Unity is not the same as uniformity. Scripture tells us that, on the contrary, unity can co-exist with diversity, as in the body. Nor is unity the same thing as union; for union can be created by men, it can even be forced.

But unity is created by God.

What Paul seems to be emphasising in verse 10 is that one of the essentials for true Christian unity is unanimity with regard to truth – 'That you may be perfectly united in mind and thought'. C.K. Barrett comments: 'Neither at this point nor later does Paul suggest that the church can be mended by ecclesiastical politics.' True unity is founded on apostolic doctrine.

There is much talk about the scandal of our divisions. But the real scandal is not that we do not all worship in the same way, nor that we do not belong to the same organisation, nor that we do not all share the same view of church government and the sacraments, nor that we do not have the same concept of ministry. The real scandal is that we do not all preach the same message.

So the first ground of our unity is *apostolic truth*.

In verse 11, Paul gives us the second ground of our unity; and it is very easy to miss it. It is in Paul's mode of address: 'My brothers'. For Paul, 'brother' is not just a convenient way of addressing someone whose name you have forgotten. It is a theological concept. When you unpack it, you discover that it contains the doctrines of regeneration and adoption, and it tells us that our unity is based on what God has done to incorporate us into His family. So if the first ground of our unity is apostolic truth, the second is *Christian brotherhood*.

Here in Corinth, unity has been fractured at the point at which it has so often been fractured; a concentration on man rather than on God (verse 12). Whatever the distinctive features of each of these groups may be is not terribly important. The significant thing is that within the one church of Jesus Christ there were rival groups quarrelling with each other over their allegiances to different men, and here again you see the fatal danger of the church becoming man-centred rather than God-centred.

Now finally in verses 13 to 17, Paul tells us that there are three things that bear witness against this man-centred division. The first is the nature of Christ, the second is the nature of the atonement, and the third is the nature of baptism.

The nature of Christ
He is One; and since there is one Christ and He cannot be divided, Christians in the same body may not be divided from each other. So Paul asks, 'Is Christ divided?' (verse 13). The implication is, that it is a preposterous idea.

The nature of the atonement
In his atoning death, it was Jesus who stood in our place, bore our sins, and received our judgement. It is our common indebtedness to Him exclusively as our Saviour which binds us to every other believer. It is he who has purchased each of us by His blood. How then can we say that we belong to Paul, or to any other man? So Paul asks, 'Was Paul crucified for you?'

The nature of baptism
In baptism we are baptised into the name of Christ, and baptism therefore becomes a symbol of our union with Christ as the One from whom all the riches of God's grace

flow. So baptism is another sign of our unity ('One Lord, one faith, one baptism', Ephesians 4:5). Astonishingly, the Corinthian Christians were making baptism a cause of division instead of unity by maximising what Christ had minimised; for instance, the issue of who had baptised them.

So Paul says in verse 14: I am glad I did not baptise any of you, with a few exceptions . . . 'so no one can say that you were baptised into my name.' He's saying, 'So unimportant is it that I can't even remember which of you I baptised, I think I baptised one or two of you.' Because that is not the most important thing.

The unity of the church is grounded on what God has said and what God has done. It is fractured by a concentration upon men rather than upon God, and it is demonstrated in the nature of Christ, the nature of the atonement and the nature of baptism.

The true unity of the church of Jesus Christ is created not by men but by God. But we can either mar it by our man-centredness, or maintain it by putting God at the centre of everything. That is the unity described so beautifully by Moulton Milligan, when he speaks of –

> All wills bowing in the same direction,
> All affections burning with the same flame,
> All aims directed to the same end;
> A unity of heart and mind and will.

May God increasingly make His church display such a glorious pattern.

2. The Wisdom of God
(1:18—2:16)

The passage to which we now turn is the fairly lengthy one which begins at chapter 1 verse 18 and goes right through to the end of chapter 2. In it, Paul is still expounding and applying the text which he quotes at the end of chapter 1, from Jeremiah 9:24: 'Let him who boasts boast in the Lord.'

As I suggested in our last study, the basic problem in the church at Corinth was that they were boasting in human achievement and were absorbed with the importance of man. That is, they were man-centred instead of being God-centred. That is the specific disease which Paul deals with in these first four chapters of the epistle.

In the first seventeen verses of chapter 1, Paul deals with this tendency by the particular emphasis of his teaching on the church of God. He relates to us that it is founded on divinely revealed truth; orginates in divinely provided grace; consists of divinely sanctified and called believers; is characterised by divinely enriched and gifted members; is destined for a divinely secured future; and is united by a divinely created unity.

And all through his teaching on the church, Paul's

emphasis is on God's initiative in our salvation, God's sovereignty in all His dealings with men, and above all God's sovereign purpose for the church.

In the passage before us, Paul shows us that the spirit of man-centredness is a gross distortion of the very essence of the Christian gospel, which exalts God and humbles man, and indeed of the whole manner in which God reveals His wisdom and displays His power. He does so with a jealous regard for His own glory.

From verse 18 of chapter 1 and throughout chapter 2, Paul touches upon four areas where God exalts His glory and excludes human boasting in the display of His wisdom.

The nature of His gospel (1:18–25)

You will notice that Paul introduces this section to us by means of a bridge passage, which is verse 17. 'For Christ did not send me to baptise' – some had been using baptism as another excuse for division, a catalyst for being fragmented in the church according to who had baptised them – 'but to preach the gospel.'

Now in verse 18 he begins to describe for us the manner in which God has displayed His wisdom and power in the nature of the gospel. The message of the gospel is described in verse 18, as the word or 'message' of the cross. And nowhere is the glory of God more fully displayed or more jealously guarded than in the cross of Christ.

The 'word of the cross' refers, according to Charles Hodge, 'to the doctrine of salvation through the crucifixion of the Son of God, as a sacrifice for the sins of men'. That is, it is God's whole method of saving sinners, by grace alone through faith alone in Christ alone. And nothing so effectively humbles the natural man – and is therefore obnoxious to him – as the full revelation of that gospel.

Notice, that a gospel which merely invites people to Jesus to sort out their problems and make them happy neither exalts God nor does it humble man. Indeed, if anything, it makes God man's servant. You can see how it happens. If our appeal is, 'Are you dissatisfied with life? – come to Jesus and He will sort you out!', we are not really preaching the message of the cross in its biblical sense.

For the message of the cross does not just deal with the symptoms of man's condition, it goes to the root of the disease and exposes man's pride, his worship and service of self rather than God, the desperate seriousness of that condition in the light of God's holy wrath and judgement, and man's utter inability to do anything about his plight. At the same time it exalts God as the only Saviour and, pointing at the cross, manifests the glory of His character. For nowhere are the love, and holiness, and justice, and truth, and compassion, and grace, and beauty, and wisdom, and power of God so clearly displayed – as in the cross of Christ.

Now it is precisely *because* God has, on the cross, so displayed His own glory and specifically excluded any opportunity for human pride and arrogance, that the cross is an offence to the natural man, whether it be to the Greek's pride of intellect or to the Jew's pride of religion.

In verse 18 there are two groups: 'Those who are perishing', and those 'who are being saved'. It is their relation to the gospel that determines to which category they belong. Those who are perishing, perish because the message of the cross is offensive to them; and those who are being saved are being saved because they have found the power of God in the message of the cross.

The great principle which Paul is enunciating is that wisdom and power for salvation are found not in man but in God; and God's purpose in the gospel is so to set forth His own power and wisdom that human power and human wisdom are not just minimised, but excluded.

Now Paul supports that principle in three ways.

The biblical argument

Paul wants to demonstrate that what he is saying is neither merely novel nor merely personal; he is eager to be biblical. That is made clear throughout this chapter in the frequent quotations from Scripture, with the formula 'It is written' (*cf.* 1:31, 2:9, 3:19).

So he quotes in verse 19 from Isaiah 29:14, and points to God's consistent practice in Scripture of by-passing human wisdom and cleverness. Salvation for Israel was never by human ingenuity. They had to learn to stand still, and see the salvation of God.

The quotation from Isaiah refers to the occasion when Sennacherib the king of Assyria was planning to conquer Judah. God told His prophet not to worry or fear, because the king's plan would fail. But it would not fail because of the strength of Judah's army, nor because of the strategy of Judah's king, nor because of the subtlety of his advisers. Judah would be saved solely by God's power, with no human help.

The contemporary argument

In the series of rhetorical questions of verse 20, I believe that the apostle is pointing to the contemporary world, and he is asking us to observe what has happened to the wisdom of men.

When you come to the real problems of mankind and to the real issues of life, and to the ultimate questions people are driven to ask, then, says Paul, where are your great thinkers? Where is the wisdom of this world? It is not that we decry what man has done, nor does Scripture have any interest in detracting from human achievement. But the question is, where has it got him?

Our technology has advanced to the point which would have been ludicrous daydreaming to our forefathers. We can control so much: we can control a man's journey into outer space and land him on the moon and bring him back again safely. But when you are facing the real issues of life, we are bound to acknowledge that while we can control a man's journey to the moon, we cannot control his behaviour here on earth. So you can have men on the moon and hell on earth at one and the same time, and we can do nothing about it. Well might Paul challenge his contemporary world, and we ours, with the questions: 'Where is the wise man?', 'Where is the scholar?', 'Where is the philosopher of this age?', 'Has not God made foolish the wisdom of the world?'

That is why it is so important for us to have our confidence in God and in God's gospel. 'For the foolishness of God is wiser than man's wisdom, and the weakness of God is stronger than man's strength' (verse 25). My dear friends, it is in the gospel of God that hope is to be found for the modern world, for it is there that God sweeps aside human wisdom and all its pretensions, and reveals His own saving power.

The theological argument

Why is it that in the gospel human pride is brought to nothing, and human wisdom is shown up in its poverty? Paul tells us that the answer is really in the sovereign pleasure of God. 'God was pleased through the foolishness of what was preached to save those who believe' (verse 21).

That is, there is in verse 21 a kind of twofold divine decree, expressed negatively and positively. Negatively, God has decreed in His wisdom that the world will never come to know Him by its own wisdom. Positively, God was pleased through the foolishness of what was preached to save those who believe. Notice the verbs in verses 22, 23, and 24. Jews 'demand', Greeks 'seek', but we 'preach' and God 'calls'.

That is, we do not respond to the demand for signs or the seeking after wisdom. We do not tailor our ministry or message to the demands and requirements of men. Instead, says Paul, we put our confidence in God and in the gospel. 'We preach Christ crucified' (verse 23). Uncrucified human pride will undoubtedly stumble over that message, just as the Jews did. The man who worships human reason will undoubtedly dismiss it as folly. But the mysterious and glorious thing is that as we preach Christ crucified, the sovereign God who draws men to Himself will draw both the self-righteous Jew and the proud Greek to experience the power and wisdom of God in the profound simplicity of the gospel.

I think we need to hear this message in a special way in the evangelical world today. For we are experiencing a crisis of confidence in God's sovereign power in salvation. We need to ask ourselves, time and time again: 'Am I absolutely clear *who* it is that saves men, and *what* it is that saves men?' It is neither human gift or wisdom, nor new methodology, nor intellectual skills. It is the power of God in the gospel of God.

And the other crisis of confidence is related to that. It is a crisis of confidence in preaching as the primary method God has ordained for proclaiming Christ crucified and for revealing His power and wisdom. There are notable exceptions, but the general picture in the church of Jesus Christ in Britain is one of a decline in biblical preaching. Such a decline is always the mark of a weakening and declining church. We therefore need to plead with God most earnestly in these days for a new visitation of His grace, in which He will raise up multitudes of gifted, godly pastors, who will feed the flock of God.

So, God exalts His glory and excludes human boasting, in the nature of the gospel. He also does so in,

The membership of His church (1:26–31)

In verse 26 Paul picks up the thought of God's calling from verse 24, and illustrates the same principle in those who made up the church of Christ at Corinth. He is really saying, 'Look around you, brethren; who are the people whom God has called and saved and brought into His church at Corinth? The answer is that according to worldly standards, not many are amongst the wise or powerful or noble. On the contrary, God has chosen those who by human reckoning were foolish and weak, low and despised. He seems to have gone out of His way to choose the nonentities in the world's eyes' (*cf.* verses 27–28).

Now why has God done this; and what is it that He is doing? The ultimate answer to that question is in verse 29. His sovereign choosing of a people in Corinth has this design; that no human being might boast in the presence of God.

God is showing that salvation is by the wisdom and power of God alone, and man can contribute nothing whatsoever to it. He will never merit or deserve anything from God other than judgement. He often chooses the foolish and weak to proclaim unmistakably that it is by His wisdom and power alone that men are saved.

Notice how the apostle hammers home this truth, that salvation is God's work and not man's. In verse 26, the saving event is God's calling me – not my calling upon Him. In verse 27 (twice) and in verse 28, Paul emphasises again that the saving fact is God's choice of me, not my choice of Him.

In verse 30, 'It is because of him that you are in Christ Jesus' – and for no other reason in the world.

Salvation has its only explanation in God's bounteous grace in Jesus Christ, who has 'become for us wisdom from God' – that is, the wisdom which produces righteousness to justify us, holiness to sanctify us, and the redemption of our bodies to glorify us. 'Christ Jesus has become for us wisdom from God, that is, our righteousness, holiness and redemption' (verse 30).

It is very clear therefore from what God has done in calling people to Himself in Corinth, that all self-glorification is thoroughly objectionable to God. He has designed the gospel and called the church in such a way as to exclude all human boasting.

But notice, the reverse of that self-glorification is not a kind of man-centred and negative obsequiousness. It is a positive glorying in the Lord (verse 31).

The ministry of His servants (2:1–5)

Here again, in this third area where God exalts His glory and excludes human pride, Paul quite deliberately contrasts human weakness and divine power, and the message is the same: that no flesh shall glory in the presence of God, neither the flesh of the sinner seeking his own salvation, nor the flesh of the preacher seeking the salvation of others. If the sinner must humble himself to receive God's Word, the preacher must humble himself to proclaim it.

The principle is illustrated both in the message he preached, and the manner in which he preached it.

Paul's resolve in chapter 2 verse 2 is to preach nothing except Christ and Him crucified; and that is of course, as R.C.H. Lenski insists, 'in no way restrictive, as though Paul presented only a portion of the gospel in Corinth and omitted other portions.' It is in fact a comprehensive summary of the entire gospel; it is Jesus Christ in His perfect humanity, His divine messianic dignity, His willing obedience to the Father even to the death of the cross, His perfect offering of Himself as a substitute for sinners, the power of His death to breach the strongholds of Satan and end the reign of sin, our union with Him in that death and in His subsequent resurrection, and the guarantee in His perfect atonement of His ultimate enthronement.

And all of that as the fulfilment of what God had spoken in the Old Testament Scripture. So to preach 'Jesus Christ and Him crucified' is to preach the whole counsel of God, and there is nothing so designed to humble man and exalt God as that.

However, not only the message which Paul preached, but also the manner in which he preached it, bore witness to the power and glory belonging to God and not to Paul. In verses 1, 3, 4 and 5, this is what he is emphasising. He clearly had a strong zeal that nothing whatsoever should distract people's attention from the centrality of God and the message of Christ crucified.

It is possible that the weakness, of which he speaks in verse 3, is a physical weakness. Paul did not, it seems, enjoy good health. Like many of God's choicest servants, he was plagued by many bodily sicknesses, and here in Corinth all that was probably compounded by the exhaustion of his experiences in Greece and by the prospect of preaching in this notoriously wicked city. Yet Paul had learned that God's strength was made perfect in his weakness, and he had learned therefore rather to glory in his infirmity.

The permanent lesson is that Paul's methodology was controlled by the same principle which controlled his message; the centrality of God instead of man, and confidence

in God which excluded a confidence in men. My Christian
friends, it is vital that our methodology be subjected to that
kind of scrutiny, and that we refuse to employ methods
which betray a confidence in man rather than in God, and
which draw attention to man rather than to God.

Paul's great concern is that through his message and the
method by which he proclaims it, what happened in
Corinth should be a demonstration of the Spirit and of
power – that is, something that could not be explained in
merely human terms.

David Prior, in his recent commentary on 1 Corinthians,
insists that this paragraph compels preachers to ask some
searching questions of themselves. Let me give you some of
them.

Is our preaching genuine proclamation? Do we obscure
our proclamation with lofty words or anything else? Have
we made a firm decision to make Jesus Christ and Him
crucified the theme of our preaching and the centre of our
living? Do we experience proper tentativeness and do we
taste our own vulnerability as preachers of the gospel in a
pagan, hostile world? Does our preaching demonstrate the
power of the Spirit? Do the results of our preaching
demonstrate the power of the Spirit? Are people's lives
being changed? Do they know the power of the Spirit in
their own lives?

There are many such searching questions we need to ask
ourselves, because I fear that due to our concentration on
man, we know little of the power of God.

The revelation of His truth (2:6–16)

All that Paul has so far been saying has had a negative
emphasis; to minimise human wisdom and worldly power.
Now he turns more positively to the way in which God re-

veals His wisdom. Verse 6: 'We do, however, speak a message of wisdom among the mature.' That wisdom is not like the wisdom of men. It has unfathomable depths, so that the more we grow into Christian maturity the more there will be for us to search and ponder in the wisdom of God.

This wisdom, as verse 7 makes clear, is really God's plan of salvation: 'We speak of God's secret wisdom, a wisdom that has been hidden and that God destined for our glory before time began.' It is hidden and secret, in the sense that natural skills do not enable us to grasp it; and the most brilliant intellects may be baffled by it, for the simple reason that it is not known by research but by revelation (*cf.* verses 8 and 9). That revelation is the peculiar work of the Holy Spirit, who searches the deep things of God and reveals them to the child of God.

Do you see the stages by which Paul traces for us the process of salvation? Let me point them out to you.

1. God the Father decrees and prepares His wisdom before time begins. The purpose He has in view is the glorification of His people. He is working out the details of His perfect wisdom in His plan for our full redemption, before the foundation of the world (verse 7). That is stage one of revelation. It begins in the secret mind and purpose of God.

2. The Holy Spirit searches the deep things of God (verses 10–11). You will notice, that no human mind, no rulers (verse 8) of this age could understand them. Now will you notice, my brothers and sisters, this thrilling thing; how when God brings the revelation that has its origins in His secret wisdom to us, He does so through the Spirit in this quite specific way?

Here is a mysterious activity which takes place within the Godhead. From human analogy, Paul points out, the thoughts of a man are only known by the spirit of that man. You don't know what I'm thinking just now, do you? I'll tell you. I'm thinking that it's four minutes to eleven. You wouldn't have known that, unless my spirit was able to ransack my mind, and then tell you. And by analogy, the thoughts of God are known only to the Spirit of God (verse 11). So the Holy Spirit searches the mind of God and plumbs the depths of the wisdom of God.

Here is a ministry of the Holy Spirit that we seldom think of. He ransacks the mind of God to bring forth the riches of His purposes.

3. What the Spirit searches, He reveals to the apostles (verse 10). Here the Spirit, having searched the mind of God, is described as revealing what He has discovered; and that revelation is specifically directed, as I believe verse 10 tells us, to the apostles. 'God has revealed it to *us*.' In the Greek, the tense of the verb is an aorist, and the words 'to us' occur at the beginning, for emphasis. I think the conclusion that scholars come to, that it is the apostles of whom he is speaking, is therefore right.

4. The fourth stage of the process is that what God by His Spirit has revealed to the apostles, He enables and equips them to understand (verse 12). Then He inspires them to speak and teach it. The result of that inspiration for us is the New Testament scriptures. Of course the Holy Spirit inspires and illumines and teaches us too, but in a different way from the apostles. As I suggested at the beginning of our first study, He inspires the apostles to write Scripture, and He inspires us to understand, teach and preach it.

5. The final link is that what the Holy Spirit reveals to the apostles and they teach, the Spirit enlightens the hearers to

hear and to accept and to understand (verse 14). In other words He gives him the mind of Christ.

What a glorious picture, my brothers and sisters, of how eager God is to teach us His wisdom! But correspondingly, how jealous God is in guarding His own glory in the whole process of revelation. At every stage we are utterly dependent upon God. It is He who decrees and decides and plans and prepares the riches of His grace.

It is the Spirit alone, therefore, who is able to illumine the truth of God to our understanding. I will tell you just one place where that would make the world of difference to our lives, and that's in the place of prayer. If only the Holy Spirit could illumine darkened minds, how differently we would see the whole place of prayer, and the revelation men and women need of the truth of God!

So the apostle says, Let him who boasts boast in the Lord. May God make us more and more that kind of people.

3. The Work of God
(3:1–17)

One of the major problems in the church at Corinth, deriving from the basic disease of man-centredness, was their false view of Christian leadership. We have been made aware of that already, in chapter 1:12, where the symptoms of this man-centred thinking about Christian leadership are that they attach themselves to men, make invidious comparisons, playing one off against another and thereby degrading and endangering the whole cause of the gospel.

It is this whole issue that Paul takes up in chapter 3, and in dealing with it he sets before us some highly significant principles for Christian service and Christian leadership. I want to identify four of them, and to take you through the chapter in the light of them, especially concentrating on the first fifteen verses. You could call these four principles 'Four Laws for Christian Service or Christian Leadership'.

The first of them I would want to put in some such form as this:

God's primary concern is with the worker rather than with the work

Or – to put it another way – God's pre-occupation is not

with our service but with our character.' There is an unchanging law in the work of God, that this is what ultimately matters. That seems to me to be what lies behind the first four verses. The root problem which distorted all their thinking and marred their service was that they were 'carnal' rather than 'spiritual'.

In verse 1 you get the terms, variously translated 'spiritual and carnal', 'spiritual and unspiritual', 'spiritual men and men of the flesh' or 'spiritual and worldly'. It is important to notice the language Paul uses. He does not here call them 'natural' men, or as in the RSV 'unspiritual' men (*cf*. 1 Corinthians 2:14 RSV).

Paul does not deny that they possess the Spirit. But he cannot call them 'spiritual men', because they are not led and controlled by the Spirit. So he uses a third term, 'carnal men', by which he means men who are indwelt by the Spirit but are apparently not controlled by the Spirit. They are living, as the NIV puts it, 'in a worldly way'.

Now it is significant that their carnality is evidenced, not in some moral sphere, but in the simple fact that they were refusing to grow up. And Paul's burden is that it is what they *were* spiritually that was going to have the most profound effect upon the whole work of God in Corinth.

In verses 1 and 2 Paul's concern is not that they are spiritual babies. All the attributes of babies are extremely attractive – in babyhood. But when they persist into later life, that becomes a tragedy. It is this persistent spiritual babyhood that Paul is speaking of, as is evident from the last phrase of verse 2: 'Indeed, you are still not ready.' The particular attribute of babyhood which he identifies is appetite. They do not have an appetite commensurate with their age.

In the physical world, that is an indication that something is radically wrong. There are only two occasions in your life when the only thing that you can eat is milk. One is when you are a baby, and the other is when you are ill. Now one of the clearest marks that there is something far wrong with you spiritually is when your appetite is only for spiritual milk. My brothers and sisters, we need to examine ourselves before God on this issue. How is your appetite? What do you look for from the ministry of God's Word? Entertainment? The mere moving of your emotions? Or solid food for your soul? I say again; how is your appetite?

Now the reason why this whole issue of spiritual maturity and growth is so important is that God is infinitely more concerned with the character of the worker than with the giftedness of his service. In the whole realm of spiritual leadership, it is what I am that matters to God, infinitely more than what I do. The prime issue in Christian leadership is, am I myself growing in spirituality?

If you think of it, that is not true for almost any other sphere of life. Most people are able to divorce their personal life from their professional competence. So people say, 'My private life is my business.' But that is a separation you can never make in the service of God, because there what a man is largely determines what he does.

I wonder whether you know that little book of E.M. Bounds, called *Power through Prayer*? If you don't, you really ought to try to get a copy and read it thoroughly. Let me quote a little of it to you.

> The church is looking for better methods, whereas God is looking for better men . . . . It is not great talents, nor great learning, nor great preachers that God needs, but men great in holiness; great in faith, great in love, great in fidelity, great for God. These men can mould a whole generation for God.

Now what Paul saw with distress and apprehension in

Corinth was that they were not producing men like that.

From an entirely different sphere, I wonder if you know Helmut Thielicke's little book called *The Trouble with the Church*? He makes this incisive comment:

> Anybody who wants to know whether a particular soft drink is really as good as the advertising man on the TV says it is, cannot simply believe the phonetically amplified recommendations, but must find out whether this man actually drinks the stuff at home, when he is not in public.
>
> Does the preacher himself drink what he hands out in the pulpit? This is the question that is being asked by the child of our time, who has been burned by publicity and advertising. The fact that [the preacher] works hard on his preaching, that he studies the Bible and ponders theological problems, this would still be no proof that he drinks his own soft drink. The question is rather whether he quenches his own thirst with the Bible, and if I see a breach, if I see no connection between his Christian and his human existence (so argues the average person consciously or unconsciously), then I am inclined to accept the conclusion that he himself is not living in the house of his own preaching but has settled down somewhere beside it, and that the centre of gravity in his life lies somewhere else.

It is that last phrase that I find so challenging. The key question is, where is the 'centre of gravity' of my life? Is it in the cause of God, the gospel of God and the glory of God? Or is it somewhere else?

It is very interesting that the particular expression of carnality of which the apostle speaks in verse 3 is jealousy and strife.

You see, one of the marks of refusing to grow up is the persistence of jealousy and strife, for the centre of baby's life is self; he expects to be the centre of everybody else's world, and if he is not, if he is very small he will scream. If he is a little older he will throw a tantrum. He wants to be the centre of the world.

Jealousy and quarrelsomeness are marks of childhood. But they are also the marks of the lives of men and women who are living as though they had never been touched by the grace of God. At the end of verse 3 and again at the end of verse 4 Paul challenges the Corinthians with this: 'Are you not behaving like ordinary men?' C.K. Barrett says that the question 'brings out clearly what Paul means by fleshliness, which is life cut off from and opposed to God; self-centred, self-contained, self-directed.

Now it is a real test of character, for me anyway (I imagine it is for you too), to ask, 'Can I truly and genuinely be glad when God is blessing and using someone else in a way that He is not blessing and using me, because my consuming passion is for the honour and glory of the name of God, and not just for my own little show?'

Adoniram Judson – he went to Burma, a great missionary – leaving Andover Theological Seminary in the United States, wrote in his journal as he sailed for Serampore, 'I crave from God such a pure zeal for His glory that I may have a holy disinterest in whom He uses, so long as the dear name of my Saviour is honoured and His kingdom grows.' Oh, that God would pour out that kind of spirit and that attitude amongst us in the church of God!

We are bound to confess that the jealousy and strife of first-century Corinth are not so far removed from the Christian church in 1985. But they are just symptoms of that basic disease which Paul diagnoses in Corinth, namely, a persistent spiritual adolescence, a refusal to grow up into true spiritual manhood or womanhood. And the seriousness of it is that in the service of God it is a man's spiritual character which is the primary issue.

Robert Murray McCheyne wrote to a young ordinand on 2 November 1840, 'It is not great talents God blesses, so much as great likeness to Jesus. A holy minister is an awful weapon in the hand of God.'

That principle applies in every sphere of Christian leadership. It does not, of course, mean that God rewards us because we are good, and withdraws Himself from us when we are not, but it does mean that there is a law in the Kingdom of God that the character of the servant matters to God above all; and therefore we need to guard our own souls.

Let me now take you on to the second principle, which could be expressed like this:

This work is God's work, not ours

Paul now goes on in verses 5 to 9 to show, within the great balance of Scripture, that although God makes much of the man in the sense of being concerned with his character, the man God uses is the man who is ready to be nothing, so that the excellency of the power may be of God and not of man. So in verse 5 Paul sets about demolishing their adulation of men. 'What, after all, is Apollos? And what is Paul?'

You will notice that Paul uses the neuter gender to emphasise his point. That is, he does not say 'Who is Paul?' and 'Who is Apollos?', but literally, 'What thing is Apollos? What thing is Paul?' Lightfoot says that 'the neuter gender is exceedingly derogatory'.

Paul answers his own question, ridiculing the tendency to make much of men: 'They are the *diakonoi*, they are only servants.' The word is not used here in any technical sense, it is really the word for a waiter at table, and later it came to be used of people who were in service generally. Leon Morris says it is a word which stresses the lowly character of the service rendered.

Now Paul is stressing this emphasis, because he is hypersensitive to anything that would detract or distract from the centrality of God and the glory of God in the work of God. 'Let him who boasts boast in the Lord' (1:31).

So Paul clarifies the place that he and Apollos had in planting the church at Corinth. They were (verse 5) 'only servants, through whom you came to believe – as the Lord has assigned to each his task'. In other words, Paul and Apollos were not the cause, but only the instruments of their coming to faith. Paul now goes on to demonstrate this with a horticultural metaphor in verse 6: 'I planted the seed, Apollos watered it.' That may well mean that Paul was the first evangelist to work in Corinth and that Apollos followed him continuing the work of evangelism and helping in the building up of the church. But Paul's point is that planting and watering are not the efficient causes of vegetation. It was God who by His life-giving power gave the growth. So (verse 7) neither he who plants nor he who waters is anything, but only God who makes things grow. C.K. Barrett adds, 'The only significance of planter and waterer is that God accepts their labour and works through them; they have no independent importance.'

The whole emphasis of this paragraph is that this work is God's work and not ours.

Left to ourselves, of course there are all sorts of things that we are entirely capable of doing. We can interest people, and even profoundly influence them. We can indoctrinate them and organise them and educate them, we can move them emotionally and convince them intellectually.

But only God the Holy Spirit can regenerate and recreate and remould and renew them, until His glory begins to appear in human flesh. Only God can do that; nobody else in the universe can. All your skill, all your gifts, all your training and all your reputation will never touch that sphere. It is God's sphere; and, my brothers and sisters, there is one thing that God will never do. He will never let you interfere in it, because He is jealous for His glory. And if you and I neglect or play down this truth, He will be displeased with us, because the Lord our God is a jealous God and He will not give His glory to another.

Recognising all this should produce two results in us, according to the apostle. In verse 7, humility before God; in verse 8, equality before one another. Two vitally important things.

Humility before God (verse 7): 'Neither he who plants nor he who waters is anything, but only God.'

Now humility is one of the most difficult things to talk about, isn't it? Yet I'm more and more persuaded that true biblical humility is one of the key elements in true usefulness to God. It does of course have to be distinguished from that false self-conscious grovelling that is always parading itself. But this fruit of true Christlike lowliness of heart is something of which you will be quite unconscious.

I think it derives basically from God being at the centre of life, instead of self. That is really what biblical humility and lowliness of mind is, and that is why it is so costly. It is not an affected thing, it is not having a diffident, retiring personality by nature: it has nothing to do with personality. It is something that flows from a deep work of grace.

Alexander Whyte had a young man preaching for him in Edinburgh on one occasion. The young man was getting a real reputation in Edinburgh as a great preacher. He had come to Free St George's in Edinburgh (as it then was), and he went up into the pulpit full of a sense of what they were all expecting from him, the young luminary.

And then something happened and his mind went a total blank. He made a dreadful mess of the whole thing, forgot what he was going to say, his mind went blank and it was a disaster.

He came down from the pulpit steps a broken-hearted man. In the vestry he cried to Whyte, 'What went wrong, sir?'

Whyte said gently to him, 'Well, laddie, if you had gone up the way you came down, you would have had more chance of coming down the way you went up.' Only God is anything, in Christian service.

But the corollary of that is not only humility before God, but also . . .

Equality before one another (verse 8): 'He who plants and he who waters are equal, and each shall receive his wages according to his labour.'

The NIV says, 'The man who plants and the man who waters have one purpose,' but the meaning seems to be that they are one in the sense of equality, and that would follow on very obviously because it is the same sinister spirit that creates a lack of humility that also creates a lack of equality. The same pride which refuses to give God His place, refuses to give my brother his place. These two men's labours are both vital and both equal, although different; and therefore neither of them must affect a superiority over the other.

But it is possible in our attitudes to refuse equality to our brother or sister, and we can affect a superiority of intellect, age, gifts or status which apart from anything else makes us grossly unteachable. Says Paul in the second half of verse 8,

'Each will be rewarded according to his own labour.' In other words, it is God who will make the assessment, and prizegiving day at the end of time is going to produce a whole lot of profound surprises.

Of course this equality does not imply similarity or identity, but it does banish a spirit of affected superiority. Paul further underlines this principle of equality in verse 9 by emphasising that the work and the workers alike belong to God. We are God's fellow-workers. You are God's field. You are God's building. This work is God's work and not ours.

That leads me to the third principle, which is enunciated in verses 10 and 11.

God's work must be done in God's way

At the very end of verse 9, the metaphor moves from the agricultural to the architectural. 'You are God's field, God's building.'

From verse 10, Paul now goes on to develop the metaphor of building: 'According to the grace God has given me, like a skilled master builder, I laid a foundation.' Although the Greek work for master builder (or expert builder) is the one from which we get our word 'architect', I don't think that he is thinking of an architect in our terms, but rather a kind of supervisor of building works. You will notice how Paul once more attributes his ministry in Corinth to the grace of God, 'According to the grace of God given to me.'

What really strikes me is the ministry that God gave to Paul here in Corinth, and the evidence of his wisdom in setting about building the church of God in Corinth according to God's specification. And it all had to do with laying a foundation. Someone else was building upon it, but that was another evidence of the parity and equality of servants of God. The evidence of Paul's wisdom was that he recognised that the primary principle of good building is the patient laying of the right foundation. If we are going to be God's fellow-workers, we will need to do God's work God's way. And God's way is that buildings are dependent upon the laying of true foundations.

It is that principle that Jesus applies in terms of character and personal obedience at the end of the Sermon on the Mount. He tells the story of two men who were building, one ignoring the issue of foundations and the other digging down patiently and persistently until he had found them. The one was a fool, the other a wise man. And the same principle applies equally in the service of God.

We don't really need to wonder what it was that Paul spoke of when he said 'I laid the foundation'; Luke tells us in Acts 18. There we read that every Sabbath Paul reasoned in the synagogue, persuading Jews and Greeks. He devoted himself exclusively to preaching, testifying to the Jews that Jesus was the Christ. He stayed for a year and a half, teaching them the Word of God. That was Paul's initial ministry, patiently laying the solid foundation of the church of Jesus Christ in Corinth.

And the significant thing about foundations is that they are hidden. They attract very little public acclaim and hardly any attention. So if your task is foundation-laying, let me press upon you that everything depends upon it and you must, in God's name, never be diverted from it. When people say, 'What's old so-and-so doing in the Lord's work these days?' and there doesn't seem to be much to show, in God's name do not be diverted if you are laying the solid foundation of which Paul speaks here, through the patient preaching and teaching of Christ in all the Scriptures. All sorts of shortcuts will be presented to you, but – Nehemiah-like – you will have to say, 'I am doing a great work, and I will not come down.'

Now that leads me to the last principle Paul presents to us.

God's work done in God's way involves great cost and corresponding reward

We are introduced to the next stage of the building metaphor halfway through verse 10: 'Someone else is building on [the foundation]. But each one should be careful how he builds.' Obviously this care is to be exercised firstly with respect to the foundation and secondly with respect to the edifice. Paul deals with the first in verse 11 and the second from verse 12.

With respect to the *foundation*, the grave danger is the possibility that someone may try to tamper with it. There is only one foundation, and it is the one which is already laid, says Paul, which is Jesus Christ. Now that foundation of the church of God is Jesus Christ as the Scriptures have revealed Him and Paul preached Him; fully God, fully man, born of a virgin, perfect in His obedience, offering the one perfect and sufficient sacrifice for the sins of men in His death, raised by the Father on the third day bodily, exalted to His right hand in glory, from thence returning one day to be the judge of all the earth.

That is the Jesus whom the Scriptures reveal and who is the foundation of the church. Therefore any attack upon the person or work of Jesus Christ is an assault upon the very foundations of the Christan church. Let me quote you some words of C.K. Barrett: 'Man has no choice in the matter of the foundation of the church, namely Jesus Christ. Paul does not mean that it would be impossible to construct a community on a different basis, only that such a community will not be the church.'

Now the second way in which the builder needs to be warned to take care is in verse 12, and it refers to building with the wrong kind of *materials*. Two ways of building, involving two kinds of materials. They are distinguished from each other in two ways. One is costly, the other is cheap. Gold, silver and precious stones are costly materials. Wood, hay and straw are cheap materials. The other distinction is that one is permanent, the other is temporary. Gold, silver and precious stones last. The fire only purifies them. Wood, hay and straw are consumed. They are only temporary.

The simple point, of course, is that building something of eternal worth is always infinitely costly. There is no telling in which way it is going to be costly for each of us, but if you are set upon building for eternal worth and for God's eternal glory, then I tell you it will cost you. Of course it is possible to build in a certain way that will impress men, and even the whole evangelical world, and yet avoid the real cost. But it will be shoddy building, and on the judgement day 'It will be revealed with fire, and the fire will test the quality of each man's work.'

Fruitful Christian service and fruitful Christian leadership is costly, in terms of time, energy (not just physical energy), and above all spiritual energy in spiritual warfare and spiritual prayer. Supremely, it is costly in terms of being ready for self and pride and self-glory and self-interest to be cast down in to the dust so that God may be everything.

Amy Carmichael, who knew more about the cost of Christian service than most people, wrote these lines, on the words 'Always bearing about in the body the dying of the Lord Jesus'.

Thy vows are on me; oh, to serve Thee truly,
Love perfectly, in purity obey.
Burn, burn oh fire; oh wind, now winnow throughly,
Oh sword, awake against the flesh and slay.
Oh that in me, Thou my Lord may see
Of the travail of Thy soul
And be satisfied.

That is the real cost of effective service. 'Death worketh in us, but life in you.'

But the cost of serving God is only one side of the story. There is an infinite and most astonishing reward for it. What is astonishing is that there is a reward at all, because of course it would be reward far beyond anything that our minds could fathom, that a poor wretched sinner should be privileged to serve the King of kings and the Lord of Glory. It is a most astonishing privilege that the eternal God should take us up and employ us in some sense as instruments of His purposes.

What this reward is, it may be difficult for us ever to understand in this world. We know that it is not salvation. Paul speaks about a reward given to some and a loss suffered by others; but in neither case is either the reward or the loss salvation itself. He makes this clear at the end of verse 15. The reward is clearly a reward for faithful service.

As to its nature, we really must remain agnostic. The loss, correspondingly, will be the loss of whatever the reward is.

But what I want to concentrate on is that the reward is not merely left until the Day of Judgement. It is projected back into our present experience. It was, I think, Dick Lucas, who once said to a group of ordinands: 'Going into the ministry is like being made Moses' mother – doing what is nearest your heart and being paid for it.'

That is the spirit that should permeate all our service. The sense of sheer wonder that God gives us such an amazing privilege as this: that we should be labourers together with God.

4. The Servant of God
(3:18—4:17)

This section of 1 Corinthians could be given the title, 'Metaphors for Christian leadership', for Paul is still writing about principles of Christian leadership and service, and he does so by employing three main metaphors.

The first is the metaphor of servanthood (4:1), the second is the metaphor of stewardship (also 4:1), and the third is the metaphor of fatherhood (4:15). It is possible to see the teaching of the whole passage as built around, and deriving from, these three metaphors.

The servanthood metaphor

This metaphor, with which chapter 4 begins, has already been used by Paul in 3:5, though the word is different. In 3:5 it is *diakonos*, which originally means a table servant, or a waiter. It stresses the lowly character of service, and it came to be the general word for servant. In the New Testament it acquired a particular significance for the office of deacon. Here in 4:1, the word is *huperetes*, which originally referred to an under-rower, the lowest galley-slave, the one rowing in the bottom tier of a ship. They were the most

menial, unenvied and despised of servants. The word came
to mean an underling of any kind.

Now that description is, in 4:1, retrospective to what Paul
has just been saying. The NIV brings that out from the
Greek: '*So then*, men ought to regard us as servants of
Christ.'

At the end of chapter 3, Paul has once more been insist-
ing, 'So then, no more boasting about men! All things are
yours, whether Paul or Apollos or Cephas or the world or
life or death or the present or the future – all are yours, and
you are of Christ, and Christ is of God' (3:21–23). The significant thing is that the verbal pyramid has Paul at the bottom, not at the top. He is listing the things that belong to the
Corinthians – 'All things are yours' – and he is doing so to
cure their boasting and to deliver them from the false way
of thinking referred to in chapter 3 verse 4: 'I belong to Paul
. . . . I belong to Apollos.'

Now, says Paul, the truth is precisely the reverse. It is *we*
who belong to *you* – 'All are yours, whether Paul, or Apollos . . .' So the minister belongs to the church, not the
church to the minister. We are not just God's servants, we
are the servants of God's people. Paul is quite clear about
this in 2 Corinthians 4:5: 'We . . . preach . . . Jesus Christ
as Lord, and ourselves as your servants for Jesus' sake.'

So we fulfil a servant role; not a master's role to domineer
but a servant's to be underlings. I have a friend who always
used to sign his pastoral letters in his parish magazine the
same way: 'Your servant for Jesus' sake.' And that is a precise description of what all Christian leaders are.

But notice that in this pyramid, although all things
belong to the believers at Corinth, they do not belong to
themselves. Verse 23, 'You are Christ's.' That is, both
Christian leaders and those they lead are together servants
who owe allegiance to Christ as Lord. And the pattern of

their service is Christ's service, 'Christ is of God.'

Some have been afraid to give this idea its full force because they are afraid of the implications of the idea of what is called 'subordinationism' – that is, somehow making Christ lower than God. But of course, in His office as mediator, Jesus does willingly subject Himself to the Father and is therefore the servant *par excellence*. So, referring to the Messiah, God says 'Behold My servant,' and Jesus says in John 14:28, 'The Father is greater than I.'

Paul makes it even clearer in 1 Corinthians 11:3, when he says that the head of the woman is the man and the head of every man is Christ, and the head of Christ is God.

That does not detract in the slightest from the full divinity and divine glory of our Lord Jesus Christ and His equality with the Father. But it does mean that Christ's pattern of lowly, obedient, single-minded, God-centred, costly service is our pattern. That is why the Servant Songs in Isaiah are such an important study for any servant of God. We are to be made in the same image.

The key metaphor for Christian leadership is the metaphor of servanthood. The badge of it is the apron; the typical posture of the Christ-like leader is kneeling, to wash the feet of those he serves.

The stewardship metaphor

This metaphor provides us with another picture of the church. It has been described as a field and a building (verse 9); here it is like a household or estate, and most householders of means had a steward who was a kind of custodian, or specially responsible servant. The Greek word is the word from which we get our English word 'economist'. The Grimm-Thayer lexicon gives this definition:

The manager of a household or of household affairs:
especially a steward, manager or superintendent . . .
to whom the head of a house or proprietor has
entrusted the management of his affairs and the duty
of dealing out the proper portion to every servant.

So the steward is related to his master in terms of total subordination and total accountability. And what is therefore required of him in verse 2 is faithfulness, that is, that the master can trust him –

a. to subordinate his own interest to the master's, and
b. to deal with his goods as one who will give account to the master.

Now from verse 1 to 13 of chapter 4 there are four ways in which Paul focusses our stewardship as Christian leaders.

The stewardship of Scripture
In verse 1, this seems to be the precise sphere of our stewardship. What God has as our Master entrusted to us is what Paul calls 'the mysteries of God'. These are of course the mysteries or secrets which are revealed by God and recorded for us in Holy Scripture. So we are stewards of God's revealed truth. That is, as it were, what has been 'put into our hands' by God; and in relation to it, we are to be totally subordinate and totally accountable to Him.

Our basic concern therefore in this stewardship is that we should rightly handle the Word of Truth, and therefore have no need to be ashamed when we meet our Master, as Paul himself urges in 2 Timothy 2:15. 'Do your best to present yourself to God as one approved, a workman who does not need to be ashamed and who correctly handles the Word of Truth.'

I think that this is what the apostle is referring to in verse 6. What Paul was eager for was that they should learn from himself and Apollos 'not to go beyond what is written'. That is, he wanted them to become the kind of men and women who, as we say in Scotland, were 'thirled' to the holy Scripture: he wanted Scripture and Scripture alone to mould their minds and thinking, to set the limits of their standards and behaviour, to be the highest court of appeal for their doctrine and for them to be submitted to it in every area of their life.

It is a glorious thing when the influence we have upon others and the lesson they learn from our lives is 'not to go beyond what is written'. This is precisely Paul's example, as he explains to the Corinthians in the second letter. 'We refuse to practise cunning or to tamper with God's Word, but by the open statement of the truth we commend ourselves to every man's conscience' (*cf.* 2 Corinthians 4:2).

Many of us are thankful to God for His men who had that influence on us in our formative years. May I bear grateful testimony today to the fact that that was the influence men like A.M. Stibbs had on me during my days as a theological student. I studied in a university faculty which was as radical and unbiblical as you could imagine. But at a number of theological conferences I met and listened to Alan Stibbs, whose whole life and teaching cried out to me, 'Do not go beyond what is written!' He was a man who was wed to holy Scripture in his thinking, teaching, preaching and living. The church of Jesus Christ in Britain today desperately needs such men in places of influence and leadership.

The stewardship of criticism and praise
I believe that this is what verses 3 to 5 are dealing with.

The fact that it is to God alone that we are accountable, and that our life and service will come under His scrutiny, should put the judgement of men into its proper context. So after saying in verse 2 that it is required in stewards to be found faithful, Paul goes on to conclude in verse 3, 'I care very little if I am judged by you or by any human court. Indeed, I do not even judge myself. My conscience is clear, but that does not make me innocent. It is the Lord who judges me.'

If you are going to be a faithful steward, then you will need to keep your ear especially attuned to God's assessment of you, not man's. That means that no Christian leader must ever become a reed shaken about by every wind of criticism and praise. Do you know those lines from that great hymn, 'Courage, brother, do not stumble'?

> Some will hate thee, some will love thee,
> Some will flatter, some will slight;
> Cease from man, and look above thee;
> Trust in God, and do the right.

Such a Godward, God-centred attitude will save us from several things.

Firstly, it will save us from becoming the victims or even the playthings of human praise or criticism ('It is the Lord who judges me', verse 4).

Secondly, it will save us from becoming the victims of an unhealthy introspection ('Indeed, I do not even judge myself', verse 3). The point is that we are not always to be taking our own spiritual pulse or temperature. We are to give ourselves to serving the Lord and to living before Him with a clear conscience and not always assessing our own spiritual condition. There is of course a vital place for that, but it can easily become something of an obsession.

But there are two caveats which need to be added to that.

It does not mean that we are to be deaf or impervious

or resentful towards anything negative that is said about us; and it does not mean that God's servants do not need encouragement or guidance.

The true stewardship of all kinds of criticism is that it should be deflected upwards to God, just as a mirror can be used to deflect light. If it is negative criticism, we need to deflect it upwards to Him and ask Him to teach us whatever He may be saying to us in it and to deliver us from being harmed by it. If it is positive praise, then we need to deflect it upwards to Him, saying, 'Whatever glory is due, Lord, it all belongs to You.'

All Christian leaders need to learn the wise and biblical stewardship of criticism.

The stewardship of gifts

There is just a word about this subject in verse 7. At the end of verse 6 Paul has been urging them regarding the stewardship of Scripture; and if they do not go beyond what is written, then they will not be tempted to take pride in one man over against another. So the stewardship of Scripture and the stewardship of gifts are linked. If our minds and spirits are ordered by Scripture, we will not take pride in one man over against another, nor will we set our gifts over against the gifts of another as though we had something to boast in.

Notice how Paul questions them in verse 7. Thomas Manton the Puritan quaintly says, 'The apostle catechiseth the boasters.' The point is that it is preposterous and ridiculous to boast in gifts that have their origin not in us but in God. Whatever gifts He has given us we are merely stewards of them, and it is the stewardship metaphor which helps us to deal with this in the right way. But since it is God who is our Master, it is not only ludicrous, it is blasphemous to rob Him of the glory that belongs to Him for the gifts He has bestowed upon us. We have not earned them, we do not merit them, we are incapable of producing them, they are not ours but God's; so how dare we boast in them?

The stewardship of suffering

It seems clear to me that the theme of the whole passage from verse 8 to verse 13 is that of suffering. There is the emotional and spiritual suffering Paul experiences as a pastor in the spiritual poverty of the Corinthians. Perhaps the most painful thing about their condition to him was the illusion about themselves under which they lived, and the complacency that they displayed. That is what Paul seeks to puncture with the sarcasm and irony of verse 8.

Spiritual poverty is one thing. But to be perfectly satisfied with it is an extreme spiritual sickness. Paul's exclamation, verse 8, has the sense 'My, but you are so easily satisfied! How quickly your appetite dies! How readily you congratulate yourselves on being rich, when in fact like the Laodiceans you are wretched, miserable, poor, blind and naked!'

It is their lack of appetite, the death of any awareness of need, that really distresses the apostle. And it does tear his soul, because these are the signs of a deep-seated spiritual malady. 'Blessed are they who hunger and thirst after righteousness,' says Jesus. The corresponding woe, in Luke's version of the Beatitudes, is 'Woe unto you who are full now.'

So Paul suffers on their behalf, agonising over their spiritual condition. Incidentally, I believe that one day they will be deeply grateful that someone did agonise over them and cared enough to do so. In your church, are there some who care enough to weep over those who are suffering from spiritual poverty and starvation but don't care themselves?

Clearly, Paul also suffered physically (verse 9). The whole picture he sees illustrated in the triumphant procession of a general after a war or a campaign. The spoils of his victory were brought in. Last of all, trailed in the dust and often in chains, were the prisoners who were on display. Paul sees the apostles thus trailed in the dust at the end of the procession, like men condemned to die.

They have been made a spectacle to the whole universe, to angels as well as to men. They have become fools for Christ (verse 10). From verse 11 we have a picture of some of the extreme physical suffering that the apostle bore for the gospel's sake; and in verses 11 and 13 Paul emphasises that this is not ancient history but their present experience.

Now the question is, how do you steward such suffering? Because it is a stewardship that God has given us. He entrusts us with many different kinds of suffering, that it may be employed for His glory. How then does Paul steward this suffering? Let me point out three things in the passage to you.

THE SOVEREIGNTY OF GOD IN SUFFERING: Don't miss that little phrase in verse 9, 'For it seems to me that *God has put us* apostles on display at the end of the procession, like men condemned to die in the arena.'

That gives us the whole perspective from which Paul views his circumstances. It is here that God's sovereignty is no dry academic doctrine. It is a divine stabiliser in the storms of life for the believer, and it brings poise and peace and assurance. 'It is God who has put us' in our present circumstances. It is that conviction which is the ground of the child of God's security, and is the perspective from which we are to view suffering and the manner in which we are to steward it.

You will recollect that this is precisely the perspective from which Jesus viewed His sufferings. When Pilate blustered and threatened Him with his authority, Jesus calmly replied, 'You could have no authority over Me except it were given to you by My Father.'

It is this conviction which Augustus Montague Toplady expresses so magnificently in the words of his hymn:

> A Sovereign Protector I have
>   Unseen, yet for ever at hand,
> Unchangeably faithful to save
>   Almighty to rule and command.
> He smiles, and my comforts abound;
>   His grace as the dew shall descend;
> And walls of salvation surround
>   The soul He delights to defend.
>
> Inspirer and Hearer of prayer,
>   Thou Shepherd and Guardian of Thine,
> My all to Thy covenant care
>   I sleeping and waking resign.
> If Thou art my Shield and my Sun,
>   The night is no darkness to me;
> And fast as my moments roll on,
>   They bring me but nearer to Thee.

So the last word in suffering is never with man but with God, and we are enabled to steward it because we are persuaded that:

> My Father's hand will never cause
> His child a needless tear.

THE HONOUR OF CHRIST IN SUFFERING: In verse 9 Paul acknowledges, 'We have been made a spectacle to the whole universe, to angels as well as to men.' But the crucial issue is what he adds at the beginning of verse 10: 'We are fools *for Christ.*'

That is the significant thing about his sufferings. They are for Christ. And if his suffering brings honour to Christ then Paul is content to bear it. Some suffering seems to be pointless and meaningless, but Paul recognises that his own sufferings as well as the blessings of his life are being taken up in the hands of God, and woven into His eternal purpose to honour and glorify His Son. That is enough for the apostle.

THE EXAMPLE OF CHRIST IN SUFFERING: This is the third perspective from which Paul stewards and views his own sufferings. Here Jesus set us the perfect example. Verses 12 and 13 really refer to suffering at the hands of others; cursing, persecution and slander. Now the question is: how do we react to it?

Well, says Paul, we follow the Saviour's example, as described in 1 Peter: 'When they hurled their insults at him, he did not retaliate; when he suffered, he made no threats. Instead, he entrusted himself to him who judges justly' (1 Pet. 2:23). This is exactly how Jesus taught us we were to steward suffering: 'Love your enemies, do good to those who hate you, bless those who curse you.'

If you want three phrases to summarise that teaching about the stewardship of suffering, they are 'from Him', 'for Him', and 'like Him'. And that links us into the third and final metaphor that the apostle uses.

The fatherhood metaphor

From verse 14 Paul explains that he is willing to exercise a stewardship of suffering on the Corinthian's behalf — because they are his beloved children.

He has of course been an evangelist amongst them. He has fulfilled the function of a teacher sent from God, but in verse 15 he is eager to highlight the distinction which makes him something infinitely more than either of these. They may have had many parents and guardians. The Greek word is *paidagogos*, which really referred to that teacher or moral guardian who operated within the domestic context. You may have had many of those, says Paul; but you have only one father. And in Christ Jesus I became your father through the gospel.

What he means is that he was intimately involved in their spiritual birth. It is significant that writing to the Galatians, Paul describes himself as their spiritual mother (Galatians 4:19). To the Thessalonians he describes himself as a gentle nurse who cared for them. The point of all these metaphors is that Paul is describing the most intimate personal relationship.

Let me point out two things about this fatherhood. Firstly, its *origins*. In verse 15, Paul says, 'I became your father through the gospel.' The implication is not only that he brought the gospel to them, but that he had actually been there to witness the miracles of regeneration and adoption into the family of God, and that gave him a unique relationship with them.

That leads me to the other thing that we need to see about fatherhood, and that is the *implications* of being a spiritual father. First of all it is important to say that it does not imply either authority or superiority. It is in this sense that Jesus forbids the use of the term in Matthew 23:9. In this sense, Paul's mode of address to his fellow-Christians is the one he uses in chapter 4 verse 6, 'brothers'.

But positively, there are several implications of spiritual fatherhood, and Paul refers to three of them here.

One is *a father's example*. That is where true spiritual authority comes from. It does not come with age, experience, education or position. Writing to Timothy, Paul says 'Don't let anybody despise your youth, but be an example to the flock.' Age does not confer authority, nor does youth disqualify from it. Only an exemplary life of true godliness confers it.

So Paul can say in chapter 4 verse 6, 'I urge you to imitate me.' Leon Morris comments, 'While in the different circumstances of today, preachers may well hesitate to call others to imitate them, it still remains that if we are to commend our gospel it must be because our lives reveal its power.'

That drives us back again to the basic principle, that people are influenced far more by what we are than by what we say.

The second implication is that of *a father's love*. It is not just a sentimental or emotional attitude of which Paul is thinking. It is the kind of love he refers to in 2 Corinthians 12:14–15, where he is not speaking of being possessive, but of being himself expendable for their sake. He did not count even his life dear to himself.

Let me say that *that* is a quality in spiritual leadership which is indispensable. 'The good shepherd gives his life for the sheep,' and thereby distinguishes himself from the hireling. Although Jesus gave His life for the sheep in a redemptive way, and we do not, we do give ourselves for them in every other way.

So like a father, we love with a sacrificial, gentle, Christlike love (verse 21).

And thirdly, *a father's faithfulness*. You will notice in these verses that combined with this deep, costly love, there is an equally deep and costly faithfulness in the way Paul deals with his spiritual children. And it is of course the mark of a father, that if anyone is going to be utterly faithful with his child it will be he.

Others will be more easily satisfied than he. But, for example, he will not be content with a spiritual life that is mere talk (verse 20). He will want to see the evidence of the power of God. So he will deal faithfully with all forms of arrogance and pride and self-interest (verses 18 and 19). If he cared for them less deeply, he would deal with them less faithfully.

Let me then summarise and conclude.

Our ministry to others must be marked by the humble submissiveness of the servant, by the wise faithfulness of the steward, and by the loving example of a father.

That means that the Christian worker must be concerned not with status or office but with service; not with his own interests but with Christ's; not with his own glory but with God's. That indeed is the core of this whole introduction to 1 Corinthians. What is at stake in Corinth is nothing less than the glory of God, and Paul's jealousy for it is just a reflection of the burning jealousy in the heart of God for His own glory. 'My glory I will not give to another.' That is why God resists the proud and gives grace to the humble.

My brothers and sisters, I believe that in a thousand ways, this is what is at stake in our generation and in so many of our lives here at Keswick. So I am bound to ask you as we close – is there some area of your life where God is being robbed of His glory?

Is there some area of your service, where He is being robbed of His glory? Do you really care for the world about us? The ultimate thing that matters to God, wherever the gospel is being preached, is that there are areas of the world, and areas of our own country, where He is being robbed of His glory; and that's the ultimate motive of evangelism.

And it's the ultimate reason that we will desperately want to let God set right in our lives whatever is wrong, so that

He may have all the glory, and so that we may become a people who will go out with that text from Jeremiah ringing in our ears: 'He who boasts, let him boast in the Lord.'

CHAINED TO THE GOSPEL (2 TIMOTHY)

by Bishop Michael Baughen

1. Sharing in Suffering for the Gospel (Chapter 1)

Have you ever been at the bedside of a great Christian who is near to death – someone who has been a tremendous servant of Christ, who glows with Christ, and is soon to be with Christ? You feel almost as if you are standing on holy ground, and you hang on every word that the person says, and you're thankful to be there.

So it is in 2 Timothy. We're allowed to enter the prison, and we feel we are on holy ground as we hear this marvellous servant of God dictate to Luke – perhaps pausing, pondering, rephrasing. We know that we are listening to the farewell of a mighty man of God.

Come with me then on these four mornings into the prison cell. Listen to Paul's word, the word of the Lord, at the end of Paul's earthly life and ministry. And I believe that as we look together, we shall see not just a Christian chained to a wall or to a Roman soldier, but a Christian chained to the gospel of Jesus Christ.

The opening greetings (1:1–2)

It's worth spending some time on the opening greeting in

verses 1 and 2. *Paul* – that's how it starts. Different from the way we write letters, isn't it? We sign our name at the end, but in New Testament times you put your name at the very beginning, and the greeting also at the beginning.

The very word 'Paul' produces in every Christian, I think, a pounding of the heart. Paul, who has meant so much to the Christian church across nearly two thousand years; a man who so loved the Lord, whose heart was on fire for the gospel, and yet a man of human physical frailty who proved the grace of God sufficient. I'm thankful that the Scriptures aren't a scroll dropped from a sort of heavenly computer, but that the Word of God is mediated through people, human beings embroiled in the race of life just like you and me – and yet people who proved the power of God.

Then the word *apostle*. It's a very special title in the New Testament. Paul takes his place alongside the Twelve as God's chosen apostle to the Gentiles; who, like the others, saw the Lord, though for him it was on the Damascus Road and through direct vision in Arabia. Though others had an apostolic task, only the Twelve and Paul had supreme apostolic authority. They are the foundation, with Christ as the cornerstone, and it is the apostolic truth which the New Testament enshrines which is the apostolic succession. It isn't people, it's the truth that's handed down from generation to generation; and this epistle is concerned about our guarding and following and sharing that truth.

There is a mistaken belief around today that the church has suffered from not having a succession of apostles. That is a gross misunderstanding of the New Testament. Paul did not appoint Timothy an apostle; and yet he quite clearly commits to him the task of carrying on the apostolic commission. The apostolic succession is not a succession of apostles, but of people entrusted with the continuing and the sharing of the apostolic revelation.

So in a very real sense this letter, though written to Timothy in Ephesus (a city which was embroiled in commercialism and paganism, just as our country is today), is of course to the church at large. It is consciously part of the Scriptures, and in that sense we bow before it in reverence.

Then take the next phrase: *by the will of God*. All of us are called to be involved in the ministry of God in some way or other, but when we are called to leadership or some particular form of service, I hope we can share this qualification: 'by the will of God'. I read a letter recently in one of the church newspapers from a clergy wife who had applied for a credit card with a major chain store. When the form asked for her husband's employer, she had put down 'God'. Apparently that wasn't enough for them to trust her, for she was turned down! But in a real sense, that is what every servant of God needs to say. Who do I serve? Not a church – not a bishop – but the Lord! He is our 'divine Director', if you like, our employer.

That is why we press the question when men are called for the service of God, perhaps in the ordained ministry; we say to them, 'Do you believe that you are called by God?' That is the fundamental question, and if you are a leader, a minister, a missionary, a junior church teacher, a Christian Union president – some form of worker in the church – I hope under God that you have the understanding that God has put you there, has called you there, and that you have that position 'by the will of God'.

It is an enormous strength and rock whatever happens. And here is Paul in prison; never again able to pioneer new churches, no more missionary journeys, about to die for his faith. And yet he is still convinced that he is what he is, and is where he is, 'by the will of God'. It's a phrase that should burn into us.

When Myrtle and I opened the letter inviting us to

become Bishop of Chester and Bishop's wife, we were stunned. We didn't eat for two days. Since those days we've prayed it through and lived through it for some three years now. And it's when brickbats and bitter letters and attacks have arrived, that we have had to come back to this fundamental truth; that we do humbly believe that God has called us to this task, and that is where we stand. And I want to plead with you, whoever you are in the service of Christ, that you lay hold of that rock 'by the will of God'. It may be that like Paul in prison, you are no longer able to do many things you did in the past; but still see that what you are and where you are is 'by the will of God'.

And yet it's an awesome responsibility. Paul can speak of himself as an apostle of Christ Jesus, and you and I are ministers, leaders, servants of Christ Jesus. We have to do these tasks not for our own satisfaction, not for respect, not for pay, not for fame, not for fulfilment – but for Christ. In the end we are going to be answerable not to our fellow-Christians and to other leaders in the church, but to Jesus Christ; and the parameters of the ministry to which we are called are set in the phrase that follows.

According to the promise of life in Christ Jesus. No Christian can cut him or herself off from social ills and evils, and all that is pounding in upon us in this world for which Christ died; but the centrality of the ministry is 'according to the promise of life in Christ Jesus'. You are not called first to be a social worker, but to be someone sharing the life of Christ. That is the pivotal force of the task to which God has called everyone in His ministry. We are primarily called to bring people from death to life, to bring them to the fullness of life in Christ, to know the Spirit's transformation, to have eternal life now in knowing God and to live a life overflowing in service and care.

And if that is to be so, if that is the driving centrality of what God has called us to, then in our own lives it must be true as well, that we are those crucified with Christ, yet alive; because Christ lives in us, and the life we live we live by faith in the Son of God who loved us and gave Himself for us. Are we such people?

Before we enter into the main line of this epistle we need to pause. I need afresh to lay my bishopric before Christ; I bid you lay your ministry in the church, whatever it may be, before Him. And as we bow at the feet of the Lord of the church, just let the greeting-words come over us like a balm of comfort. Verse 2: *grace* – all the wonder of being in Christ, of full and free salvation and of the undeserved love flowing to us; *mercy* – to Paul the blasphemer of Christ, and to us, the greatest miracle of all – that you and I are converted and in the family of God; and *peace*, the wholeness of mind, body, spirit and soul as Christ makes us fully His.

It's a marvellous start to a letter, isn't it?

Paul's deep concern for Timothy (1:3–18)

Now let's feel with Paul his deep concern for Timothy. Timothy was never an extrovert or a strong personality. He'd never found it easy to be a Christian leader, particularly when the going was rough. He had a natural tendency, which you and I share, to duck out of problems, suffering or controversy. Probably he was even weak on commitment.

I suggest to you that there are five ways of strengthening which Paul presses home in this chapter.

Strengthening by reminder (1:3–7)
Paul reminds Timothy of three facts. Firstly, in verses 3 and 4 he reminds him that *he, Paul his spiritual father, is deeply concerned for him*. Now we all need and welcome encouragement, but particularly welcome is encouragement from

a parent to a child. The 'Well done' of Mum or Dad is like pure gold. The fact that your father and mother are interested in what you are doing is a great thing. And here it is Timothy's spiritual father who is interested and concerned about his son in the faith.

It is a concern that every one of us with responsibilities of ministry needs to show. The concern for people away from home, such as young people going off to college in the most exposed moment of their whole life, when every constraint from home has gone – the concern that takes a moment to pray, to write, to show you care. How Timothy's heart must have thumped into his throat as he read Paul writing 'I thank God, Timothy, as I remember you' (*cf.* verse 3). Wow – Paul remembering me and thanking God for me! Believing that God is actually at work in me!

That is a marvellous encouragement. Paul, this giant in Timothy's eyes, is actually somebody who thanks God for him. He is on Paul's prayer list, on Paul's praying heart.

People say to me, 'How on earth do you cope as a bishop?' The answer is: only by the grace of God in response to the prayers of many people. If you are one of those who pray for us, thank you. It always moves me deeply that the two vicars under whom I grew up as a boy still pray daily for Myrtle and myself; and it also moves me deeply that John Stott, who has always been to me a tremendous man of God, of inspiration and care, prays for Myrtle and myself daily in the midst of all that he has to do.

You see, it's more than sentimental encouragement. It is more than a reminder of the deep desire that we should run well for Christ – although it is all of these things; but it is a means of the grace of God in answer to prayer. Timothy will be strengthened by the reminder that Paul's heart aches for him in the bonds of deep love, and is expectant of his service for Christ.

Another reminder, in verse 5, is of *his mother and grand-mother who showed him the faith*. Timothy's upbringing had been somewhat unusual. His father, as Acts 16 tells us, was a Greek, and his mother was Jewish. It's likely she was excommunicated from Judaism for marrying a Gentile, and that seems to be confirmed by the fact that Timothy wasn't circumcised as a child. So obviously there was a problem.

It's clear that his mother still had a living faith, and that was something that came through to Timothy. On the other hand, there must have been problems in the home. This has all been a strong influence on Timothy.

I want to encourage some of you who are parents and may have teenage – or older – renegade children. In the years I was ministering at All Souls Langham Place, time after time I met young people who had renegaded against Christ and their parents for years, and had then come back to the faith; and part of the reason was the anchor of faith that had been built in the early years.

A 'sincere faith' – Timothy could look at his mother and grandmother and know that they didn't just say it but they meant it. The way they lived, and relaxed, and enjoyed and shared life – it's a far fuller thing than just going to church or reading the Bible or praying. It's something that shines through, and this had been a marvellous strengthening to Timothy. And it is to be a strengthening now, all these years on, to think back to all that he's learned and found in what was a one-parent, or one-believing-parent, family.

Thirdly, the reminder in verses 6 and 7 is of *the gift of God for ministry*. The New Testament order is quite straightforward. It is not 'I have a gift; what can I do with it?', but 'God has called me to a task and He will equip me for it.' It is always that way round, though sometimes it comes as a sort of package, such as when in Ephesians 4 the gifts of the ascended Christ are apostles, teachers, prophets

– the person together with the gifts.

I wonder whether, in your particular church, you see your ministers as a gift from God? In some denominations they are more gift-wrapped than in others, but they are a gift from God!

Paul can remind Timothy of his particular gift received through the laying on of hands (verse 6). This is mentioned in the previous epistle: 'Do not neglect the gift you have, which was given you by prophetic utterance when the elders laid their hands upon you' (1 Tim. 4:14). The laying-on of hands is normally a sign of prayer to God, it is normally in response to commitment; and the two things come together – commitment and God's grace – be it in baptism, confirmation, healing or ordination. And this is the force of it here; that Timothy's commitment to the task was matched by the church laying on hands and seeking the grace of God to equip him for the task to which God had called him.

That's the important point. You respond! It's no good waiting for the right gifts. They come when you respond to the right task. So Paul reminds Timothy that this is what God has done, and you can't go and bury such a gift in the ground; so the phrase here is 'rekindle the gift' – the NIV has, 'keep it fully aflame'.

How do you do that? Well, by recommitment and fresh dedication. By reflection, by prayer, by devotion, by using the gift and proving God's grace, and training to be a better user of the gift. To try to fulfil the ministry to which He has called us without the gifts He has given us for that ministry is stupidity and gross carelessness. It is fatal for effective ministry.

So here is a reminder that whatever the opposition, the materialism of his society, his own immaturity, ill-health, shyness, even over-protection by his mother, Timothy is

Christ's man, called by Him and equipped by Him, and he is to keep that equipment fresh.

For – verse 7 takes us on – he has not been given a spirit of timidity but of *power* – that enables us, gives us boldness, helps us endure, means we can triumph even in weakness; and of *love* – agape, self-giving love that thinks of others and does not count the cost; and *self-control* – 'self last, God first, His glory our consuming aim'.

So these are three reminders for Timothy: his spiritual father's expectancy, his spiritual upbringing – and if you weren't brought up in a Christian family, then give thanks for those who did show you Christ, who were your substitute family by the Lord's grace – and the equipment for ministry.

Strengthening by challenge (1:8–11)
In verse 8 Paul challenges Timothy, and you and me, to be prepared to suffer for the gospel. He regards it as inevitable that those who share the ministry of the gospel will suffer – 'therefore I suffer as I do' (verse 12).

Today many Christians are obsessed with avoiding suffering. They seem to be blind to the New Testament theology of suffering, and the result is an unbalanced Christianity with disastrous effects. The Corinthian church despised Paul because he suffered; they said he couldn't be a genuine apostle because of all he'd been through. In 2 Corinthians Paul blazes back at them. That is why it is such an important letter to the church today, and why my commentary on it is called *A spiritual health-warning to the church*.

I hope that you will agree with me that suffering is at the heart of the gospel, because the cross is at the heart of the gospel. All who follow Christ are not told that they will have a painless picnic, but are called to deny themselves, take up the cross, and follow Christ.

Look at verse 8 and see what Paul says. He describes himself as 'His prisoner'. What does he mean by that? After all, he's the prisoner of the Roman guard; but he looks beyond that, and says 'No. If I'm here within the will of God, I'm His prisoner.' He can actually look at his cell and see it as where Christ wants him to be – and accept it.

Christianity is assuring, it's wonderful, it's transforming with grace and faith and power and glory; but at the same time, it is challenging, daring, demanding, courageous and costly even unto death. And you and I cannot opt for just half of it. We can't be so blinkered about the question of suffering for the gospel, or so blinkered about the grace that God gives us in the midst of that suffering, that we live as a sort of 'half-cocked' Christian. And, if you look at verse 8 again, you'll see Paul's answer. It isn't just 'sharing in suffering' and it isn't just 'putting up with suffering for the sake of the gospel'; it is 'take your share of suffering for the sake of the gospel' – and then the next five, vital, words, 'in the power of God'.

Thus this very experience is turned into testimony. That marvellous phraseology of 2 Corinthians – you know, 'We're knocked down but not knocked out . . . we're perplexed but not driven to despair' (*cf.* 2 Cor. 4:8–12) – that is the secret of the power of God in the midst of what we have to endure as Christians.

Let me ask you – have you ever been tempted to be ashamed of the gospel? If your answer is 'No', I don't believe you! There are very few Christians who haven't at some time found it difficult to stand up for the gospel, particularly when they are being laughed at. Now Paul tells Timothy in verse 8 'Do not be ashamed'.

He says that because it's very easy to be ashamed. And when he asserts himself in Romans 1 or in verse 12 of this chapter and says 'I am not ashamed', he's not saying it out of bombast. He's had to fight his way through to that position.

How easy it is not to defend our faith! And yet many Christians are very courageous. Recently a music critic was dismissed who had savaged Cliff Richard after a concert appearance; the critic described his statements about Christ and the gospel as 'totally absurd'. It takes courage to stand for the gospel like that, and whenever we're tempted to be ashamed of the gospel, we need to remind ourselves of the unique and transforming truth of the gospel.

So this is how Paul proceeds, in verse 9 and 10. He gives us what is possibly an ancient hymn or creed. He speaks of the action of God 'who saved us' – don't be ashamed of that word. People still know what it means, and that's what it means for us. Snatched from disaster by the grace of Christ.

Why are so many people ashamed of the word? Jesus is called the 'Saviour' of the world. He came into the world to save us from our sins. It is indeed a word we need to proclaim. 'Who saved us and called us' – a holy calling, to be like Him – 'not in virtue of our works' – by grace, not works; 'in virtue of his own purpose', part of His divine plan from the beginning. The abolition of death, of the spiritual death. 'And brought life and immortality to light through the gospel' – with Christ the floodlights come on, and we see what it means to say that death has lost its sting, that the grave has lost its power, and that all in Christ have eternal life with Him. Immortality! – who we are, made perfect in Him. And all this 'through the appearing of our Lord Jesus Christ'; rooted, grounded, assured in Him, because it's achieved by Him.

Now, that is the gospel; and if you ever start to be ashamed of the gospel you need to rehearse what the gospel is. There is nothing to be ashamed of, because it is eternal truth that will be vindicated, and you stand upon what God Himself has done.

However, it's a truth the world doesn't want. So in verse 11 Paul emphasises that 'for *this* gospel I was appointed . . .'

'Do you not see,' says Paul to Timothy, 'that the gospel is the only answer for mankind? It's worth all the effort, the tiredness, the slog, the mockery, the persecution; so, Timothy, don't avoid the gospel to avoid suffering, but share the gospel, whatever the cost.' And he says it to all of us in the same way. Do you really want a comfortable, snug, self-indulgent Christianity? If you do – how dare you say you still believe in the gospel! Or do you really believe in it so much that you are prepared to work for it, pray for it, share it by life, and lips, and commitment; and to accept the 'therefore' of this verse, that you will suffer if you do?

Strengthening by assurance (1:12)
Verse 12 is one of the great gems of Scripture. Notice what Paul does. He lifts Timothy's eyes from the gospel to the Lord of the gospel, and thus to the guarantor of the gospel – as Paul puts it in Romans 8: if Christ is the judge, who can condemn?

So the text is not '*in* whom I believed,' but '*whom* I have believed.' 'In whom' is an arm's-length relationship, but 'whom' springs from the closeness of devotion to Christ. How often has one seen in one's ministry people who after perhaps forty or fifty years in the church have by the grace of God come to trust Christ for the first time. They will say things like, 'It's incredible! I've been in the church, on the Parochial Church Council, an elder, a deacon or something of that sort and only now at the age of fifty-six have I come to know Christ . . .'

Now that is the movement from 'in whom' to 'whom'.

Knowing the Lord is the way in which the assurance of the gospel is proven to our hearts, and however the world mocks and ignores, the gospel is for ever. It will be vindicated in the final day as the power of God for salvation, and it is because of the 'whom' we trust that 'he is able to guard until that Day what has been entrusted to me' (verse 12) – and to us. Because it is His gospel.

Strengthening by command (1:13–14)

There are two commands in verses 13 and 14: 'follow', and 'guard'. What we are to *follow*, in verse 13, is 'the pattern of the sound words'. The phrase means a sort of architect's sketch, showing the main fabric of a building, not just the finishing touches. Paul is saying to Timothy, and he is speaking as an apostle, that the foundations of the building are fixed for ever. They are non-negotiable. It is what is sometimes called the *kerygma*; that is, the central truths of the faith.

The external bricks of the building – perhaps in the form of church expression and structures, worship, details – may vary. But the central girders and foundations are for ever! Do you believe that? You see, in today's controversies that is what is at issue. What is non-negotiable? What is external?

Though some things can be altered or disposed of, you cannot disagree on the fundamental facts. They are fixed for ever, and this is the pattern that Timothy is committed to follow. But let's see that it's not simply in a cold credal form (though the creeds are important); if you are going to follow in this pattern, you are to do it 'in the faith and love which are in Christ Jesus'.

The truths of the gospel are living truths, brought about by Jesus Christ in His incarnation, in His atonement, in His resurrection and in His ascension, and by the Holy Spirit poured out upon the church. The churches that are growing are those that are taking Christ seriously, and His Word seriously, and are living these out with daily faith and love and reality. That's the answer to the academic arguments! And when I hear people saying that if you leave these basics behind then you can have an adventurous faith, it seems to me like the adventure of going into the Everglades in Florida. You're exploring in a swamp, and sinking steadily all the time. Once you've left the foundations, once you've moved your feet off the rock, once you have dismantled the girders – there's nothing left.

We are not only to follow but (verse 14) to *guard*. There have always been attacks on the gospel. All Christian leaders, not just bishops, are called to be guardians of the faith. Today many attack the gospel by arguing that as modern man cannot accept the gospel preached in the New Testament, it will have to be altered into something that modern man *can* accept. What nonsense! It sounds very plausible, especially to the non-Christian; but blindness towards the gospel is not the fault of the gospel but of the eyes.

So if you believe that the gospel is encountering barriers in today's society, you don't alter the gospel. You don't blame its author. You seek more powerfully and prayerfully to remove the barriers from people's eyes, because the gospel is the dynamic power to salvation for all who believe, in every generation. As people seek to subtract from it, or add to it, or alter it – we must hold on to it. There is no other gospel (as Paul reminds us in 2 Corinthians 11). He entrusts Christian leaders with defending it, not by shouting slogans but (verse 14) with the help of 'the Holy Spirit who dwells within us'; in the warm, pulsating power and love of the dynamic Holy Spirit.

Finally, though we have no time left to expound it, there is –

Strengthening by example (1:15–18)

You can see for yourselves the contrast between the
unfaithful, who turned away from Paul, and the faithful,
like Onesiphorus, who has persisted, searched him out on
visits to Rome, and keeps coming back. The key verse is
verse 16: 'he was not ashamed of my chains'. And this is
meant to be an encouragement to Timothy not to be
ashamed of Paul, nor of the gospel, nor of suffering for it.

So here are five great strengthenings for Timothy, for you
and me, for the whole church; to take hold of afresh, especially if you believe you are called by the will of God in service for Christ. In faith, love and by the power of the Holy
Spirit I bid myself and you to share the gospel, and if necessary to suffer for it, for the sake of Jesus Christ and for His
eternal glory.

2. Strong in the Grace of Christ
(2 Timothy 2:1–13)

The Bible is full of surprises. Quite often we expect something to happen in a particular way and it doesn't; and we're taken aback. For example, at the beginning of the first chapter of Joshua we read 'Moses my servant is dead.' But the Bible surprises us, for the next words are not 'Sit down and be upset', but 'Arise, go over this Jordan . . . . I will be with you . . . . Be strong and of good courage' (Josh. 1:2,5–6). God's purposes in the world are historically mediated through people, but they do not depend upon them. When Moses dies, Joshua is not merely to step into the breach, but is to prove the same grace of God that Moses knew.

Be strong (2:1)

Timothy is like Joshua. Paul is about to die. The thought of being without him must have been overwhelming to Timothy, and hence the force of this epistle. And what is God's statement? 'Paul my servant is about to die – "you then, my son, be strong in the grace that is in Christ Jesus." You are stepping into the breach, and you are to prove the God of Paul to be the same God for Timothy, and for every

Christian.'

It was while preparing to give the Bible readings on Moses at an OICCU conference that I was forced by the Word of God to consider these matters. It revolutionised my ministry. I found myself forced to answer such questions as: Do I believe that the God who brought Moses through the impossibilities of being in Egypt, crossing the Red Sea and taking all those people through the wilderness, is the same God I worship through Christ Jesus? If I do, then I cannot go on acting as though I am cooped up in the wilderness with no way through it. He is my God.

It's no good reading other people's biographies, unless you believe that the same God is able to work through you, that His grace can be sufficient for all who follow and serve the Lord, that we too can be strong in the grace of Christ. Do you believe that?

There are lots of people who have been converted and have turned to Christ and believed on Him, but they're always living off other people's experiences. They are dependent on a famous preacher, or a diet of paperback sensationalism that can't be followed up, and never move into that position where they themselves draw on the grace of Christ in the life and ministry to which He has called them. And God bids Timothy to move into that position, and prove 'the grace that is in Christ Jesus'.

So the exhortation in verse 1 is not mere rhetoric or back-slapping. It's not 'Be strong' in the sense of the stiff upper lip, public school tradition. It is the climax of all that has been argued in what we have as chapter 1, though of course there were no chapters in Paul's original. As we have seen, Paul has built up the strengthening of reminder, of challenge, of assurance, of command and of example, all leading up now to this statement 'Be strong'. Timothy is to take on the task. He must prove firsthand the grace that is in

Christ Jesus.

Many of us were brought up, in our early Christian lives, on some of the great texts on this theme. 'I can do all things in him who strengthens me' (Phil. 4:13), or 'Be strong in the Lord and in the strength of his might. Put on the whole armour of God . . .' (Eph. 6:10–11), or 'My grace is sufficient for you, for my power is made perfect in weakness' (2 Cor. 12:9). Made perfect in weakness! It's amazing, another surprise of the Bible; weakness is no excuse, God revels in it to show His strength. And I believe that it's vitally important for Christians (and particularly to my younger brothers and sisters in Christ) to rediscover that pounding theme of the New Testament: that it is in Christ that you find your strength.

And may I say, the Holy Spirit enables you to trust Christ in this way. He never makes Himself central, He always puts Christ in the centre, and so must we. Whenever you hear anybody making the Spirit central you know that they are off-centre, because the Spirit is always commending Christ to us, and it is through *Christ* that we can do all things, as He strengthens us.

So verse 1 is an 'I can' statement. 'We can't' is a phrase only to be used in the Christian church with caution and after much thought. It ought not to roll off the tongue immediately there's a challenge. How quickly we say 'can't'! It's the last thing that we ought to say without thought and care, because God is a God who says 'We can'.

So, be strong. The command is to be strong and to be strengthened; the expression can be used in both ways. As we hunger for God, so He meets us in grace and strength. If we don't abide in Him and He in us, we remain weak, like hungry people sitting in a banqueting room too lazy to reach out for food; like thirsty people lying by a fountain, too lazy to reach out and drink.

Christians can actually starve spiritually in this country, when we have a surfeit of helps to the spiritual life which many parts of the world would regard as sheer riches, compared with the few books that they can get hold of. The riches are all around us, and if you don't feed and think and grow in the Christian faith then you're a fool. But you're more than a fool, you're denying all that God wants to do for you.

The food is all around us, the fountain is around us; feed and drink. But it's more than that. Being strong in the grace of God isn't just waiting until you're strong enough to go out; it's going out into the waters and finding that they recede. It's when you put the foot forward that the power of God enables you. If you wait until you always feel strong enough to serve, you'll wait for ever.

Share in God's strategy (2:2)

One of the results of being strong will be the power to plan for the future in expectation of what God is going to do.

We are often really like sheep. If you watch a sheep you'll find that it is only interested in what is in front of its nose. That's how it gets lost! When you have your nose down on the immediate things, you lose sight of the greater purposes in which you are taking part. And how often God has to say to us, 'Come on; get your head up; realise who you are; realise the greater purposes into which I've called you. Head up! Head up!'

That is what God is saying to Timothy here. 'Don't just droop your hands and say, "What on earth is going to happen next?"'

What is going to happen next is what God wants to happen, and you're part of it, so get your head up and get on with it.

God's strategy stretches to the end of time and beyond. If we are to be effective for Him, we need to seek, pray for, understand and follow His strategy. That is the burning question to which your leadership has to hammer out a solution and then obey. 'Lord, what do *you* want to do?'

But some strategic principles will never change and will always be part of God's strategy, and here is one of them in verse 2. It is the strategy of teaching others, who can teach others, who can teach others, and so on *ad infinitum*. If that strategy had not been followed, you would not be a Christian and neither would I, because people who taught us were taught by other people, who were taught by other people, back to the beginning. The strategy of the Christian church is to train people who can train others – a strategy that never changes.

So look at the progression in verse 2. 'What you have heard from me' – the apostle handing on the apostolic truth – 'before many witnesses'. 'Witnesses' is a very important word, especially in light of the current controversies. We believe that the central truths of the Christian faith as we have them are truths hammered out before witnesses. Paul was not handing on some secret tradition, to know which you had to be in the inner circle. Before many witnesses God broke into the world, showed His glory, worked out His saving purpose; not in a corner, but on the public stage of the world. This is the marvellous truth that we have, and this is what Timothy must 'entrust to faithful men' – underline 'faithful' rather than 'men'. It is the apostolic succession of the truth, and faithfulness is vital.

You see, if you entrust this truth to unfaithful men, what happens? It is destroyed or twisted. If they hand it on to others it becomes more twisted and distorted until people are destroyed. So it's not enough just to teach. It's important to teach people who are faithful in teaching it to other people. In 2 Corinthians (you'll have realised which is my favourite epistle!) Paul says time and time again, we're not people fooling around peddling a Word. We're people who have renounced disgraceful, underhanded ways, and declare the truth.

So it's faithfulness which is underlined in this verse. And Paul knew only too well what had happened with unfaithful, false apostles in Corinth. He knew those prophets which, as John warns us in his first epistle, have to be tested. There are all sorts of them around. Many of those who were around in New Testament times didn't have to live with the damage they caused; and that is true today.

Not only are these men to be 'faithful', they are to be 'able to teach others also'. Of course this was Jesus' own principle. He withdrew largely from public ministry after the halfway point of his own work, to teach the Twelve, to concentrate on explaining and deepening their understanding. Once they had acknowledged who He was, then He concentrated on training them.

It is what is often called the 'nucleus principle', and it's vital for every church in the land. A church that doesn't train its people is committing suicide. Training and training programmes are of tremendous importance, even in the smallest church. When a minister says to me 'I'm too busy, I haven't got time to train', I say, 'You are ignoring a basic strategy of the New Testament pattern, that you must give time as Jesus did. He could have said that there were hundreds of thousands waiting to hear Him preach and see Him do His miracles and show forth the power of God; but instead, He sat down with the Twelve and trained them. And that is why, when He went back to glory, the church went forward in the power of the Spirit.'

My brothers and sisters, I cannot underline it strongly

enough. The church in recent generations has largely ignored this truth, to its own great cost. Now, steadily, we're understanding it more fully, we're once again understanding the principle of every-member ministry and so on. But we all need to be prepared to train and to become more able to entrust the truth to others.

'God's strategy, young Timothy, is committed to the gospel until the end of time.' And we must share in that commitment.

Four qualities of those strong in the grace of Christ (2:3–7)

In verses 3 to 7 we have four qualities that God expects to find in those He calls to teach and to lead and to serve. And the first is,

Commitment (2:3–4)
What is the aim of a soldier? Verse 4: it is 'to satisfy the one who enlisted him' – or, as one translation puts it, to be always at his commanding officer's disposal. It is a personal aim, and Paul echoes it in 2 Corinthians 5:9 – 'We make it our aim to please him.'

Now that is the driving force of commitment. I'm not first committed to Christianity, or to the Church of England. Our commitment must first be to Christ, and that goes beyond our denominational affiliation and everything else. That is what makes all the difference.

I was called up into the army by conscription. At first sight our sergeant-major looked terrifying. But he was a marvellous man – one of the greatest I ever met in the army – and in those first six weeks of our initial training, he inspired us with a love for him like a child's towards its father. When we came to our passing-out parade he was the man we wanted to please. Not the brigadier with his red hat, but the man who'd inspired us.

It was the personalising of what it meant to be a soldier that made the difference. And it is the personalising of what it means to be a soldier of Jesus Christ that makes us say that 'our aim is to please him'. I have to say it to myself a thousand times a year, when the brickbats and the criticisms come at me – people telling me I'm unsound and all the rest of it; in the end I'm answerable to Christ. Not to man, not to the Church of England, but to Christ.

COMMITMENT IN OBEDIENCE: Now if we're going to satisfy, we satisfy by obedience if we're soldiers. That is true in commitment too. Christ wants us to have an unquestioning allegiance to His authority. What makes a good soldier is his saying 'Your will be done.' I believe that one of the great heresies of the present day is that saying 'Your will be done' is a cop-out. That is a complete reversal of the New Testament! '*Your* will be done' is the deepest commitment of faith. How else can you explain Gethsemane? Do you think that Christ was copping-out when, as the sweat fell from His face like drops of blood, He said in agony '*Your* will be done'? After all, the world wants to manipulate Jesus to its own purposes. As a non-Christian, if you're going to pray it's for health or to pass exams or something like that. But tragically some Christians too treat God like a genie in the lamp. You rub the lamp and the genie appears and says 'What is your will?'

And we sometimes treat God as if He's there to do our purposes, as if He says to us, 'Yes, Master, what do you want?' But in the New Testament it's the other way around. Of course He's there to meet us in saving grace and love. That is the glory of being in His family. But commitment means coming to Him and saying 'Yes, Master; what do *You* want?

COMMITMENT IN SUFFERING: That is the commitment of the

soldier. But saying above all else 'Your will be done' involves a readiness to suffer. So verse 3: 'Take your share of suffering as a good soldier of Jesus Christ.'

Soon after I came to the diocese of Chester, we celebrated the 200th aniversary of the birth of Bishop Heber. I found it a most moving experience to research the history of this man, who was the author of the hymn 'From Greenland's icy mountains', and was brought up in our diocese.

He was about thirty-three years old when he was asked to go out to be the Bishop of all India – actually Bishop of Calcutta, but the diocese was the whole of India including what was then known as Ceylon. He delayed for several months before responding because he was young, married, with a small daughter. He knew as well as anybody that to go out to India at that point was almost certain death.

After a few months he went to India. His address to the clergy soon after his arrival is something that ought to be published. He knew what the expectancy of life was in India. His first journey around his diocese took nearly a year. He actually died within three years. His successor lasted six months. How many men and women would do that today?

Well, there are many, thank God, but there are many who wouldn't. At about the same time as the Heber anniversary I had quite a backlog of parishes needing incumbents, and I began to find the choosiness of a number of people in the ministry today quite staggering. In one of the toughest parishes in my diocese I went through thirteen men. I began to think I would end my episcopate with the name of that parish written on my heart. One person in the parish wrote to me and said, 'Has this become a no-go area for the Church of England?'

And eventually I stood in that parish with a young couple who had a babe in arms, and at the end of the day they said to me: 'Well, we can't get away from the fact that we believe that this is where God is calling us – though it's the last place we'd ever choose.' Is it any wonder that God blessed their ministry? And now they are assisted by a man who was a doctor and is now ordained; he and his wife live in an ordinary council house on that toughest estate on Merseyside, for Christ.

At the same time I found people – evangelical men, I tell you – turning down vicarages because they didn't like the *house*! I began to ask myself, what on earth has happened? What is this softness that's come in? Another man on the Wirral had almost completed arrangements for a new curate to come from theological college, and he rang one evening to finalise it; and two hours later the man rang back. 'Oh – I've just found out that your parish is on Merseyside, and my wife won't come to Merseyside.'

It's a long, long, long way from 2 Timothy 2.

Now I tell you that most aren't like that. I happened to have a run of people at the beginning such as I haven't had since. But I want to say to every younger man and woman, and indeed older ones too; if you're called to Christian service, then read 2 Timothy 2 until you can take it to your heart that you're ready to be committed, even with suffering. Living on Merseyside is pretty easy compared with going to Calcutta two hundred years ago. What we need are men and women with the guts to say to Christ, '*Your* will be done; and we're prepared to go and do that – wherever, whatever, we don't rule anything out.' (I know – because I was the same – that some of you would rule out ordination or missionary work because you think that's for people in stained-glass pyjamas! But God calls ordinary men and women, so don't rule it out.)

COMMITMENT IN SINGLE-MINDEDNESS: If you're going to be committed in this way, as the soldier has to be – ready to suffer – then (verse 4) you cannot be 'entangled in civilian pursuits'. The word in Greek is *empleko*, from which we get our word 'implicated'. It's like when your hair gets so knotted-up you can't get a comb through.

It doesn't mean that we must avoid our family responsibilities, or have no hobbies and responsibilities; these are of course important. But it means we must not be so entangled that we cannot go where, and do what, our commanding officer requires. That's the force of it. So in the Ordination Service of the Church of England we say to those being ordained, 'Apply yourselves wholly to this one thing, and draw all your cares and studies this way.'

Inside and outside Christian circles, the phrase I hear today is 'Young people will not commit themselves to anything.' Well, I hope that's not true of any young person in this tent.

Determination (2:5)

In verse 5 we have the illustration of an athlete. Determination: to reach the tape, to run the race, to do one's best to obtain the prize.

We have a race to run, and it has to be 'according to the rules'. In the Olympics the athletes had to say on oath that they had undergone constant training for ten months. Athletes show many Christians the meaning of determination. There are swimmers who actually get up at five in the morning to swim for two or three hours while the pool is quiet – and some Christians can't even have a quiet time before they go to work! If you really mean business for Christ there will be a determination to run for Him, to buffet the body, to train daily in spirit and mind and heart, and have that all-consuming passion to run for Christ in the holiness that is vital to the Christian race.

Hard work (2:6–7)

Then in verse 6 we have the picture of the farmer. There's often little glamour or excitement in farming, in all weathers, particularly in winter. It's hard work to be a farmer; and it's hard work to serve Christ. It's a wonderful privilege – but it's also hard work.

It's not just hard work; of course, it's hard work with prayer. But it's hard work nevertheless. It's that rhythm that the New Testament has of what I sometimes call the Christian's daily exercises – knees bend, coats off, knees bend, coats off, prayer, work, prayer, work, all hand in hand. And it is this hard work that Paul has shown in his own commitment to the gospel, in sowing and watering and reaping and pioneering and contending and defending.

And (verse 7) 'It is the hard-working farmer who ought to have the first share of the crops.' Little is achieved in the work of Christ without hard work, and there's a lot of laziness around in Christian circles. So Paul says 'Think over what I say'. Let him say that to us.

Endurance (verses 8–13)

Finally, Paul writes of the quality of endurance. Let me underline, this is the key word in these verses, it is a major word of the New Testament; *hupomone*. It means literally, to stay behind, not to run away when the fight is on; a good modern word would be 'stickability'.

It's not a word that's very common in today's Christian vocabulary, but it's very much a New Testament word. Peter knew it in the context of persecution (1 Pet. 2:20). James knew it (Jas. 5:11) – it's 'hupomone' men who have endured. John knew it in the context of persecution, at the same time as this epistle was being written; here is a call for the endurance of the saints, 'those who keep the commandments of God and bear testimony to Jesus' (Rev. 12:17).

John knew that it was persecution which sought out the Christians who were strong in Christ, and those who were not.

May I say again – particularly to younger Christians, though it's not restricted to them – that there is in some Christian circles and Christian Unions today what I regard – I think under God – as trivia. Christian Union meetings concerned with people who have an ache in their arm or their leg. Can you imagine Paul, in his prison cell in Rome, writing this epistle and writing about that? Is he concerned about aches? He's concerned about Christ, and about commitment.

Endurance is a word that for many means effort and strain rather than triumphant grace, but it is one of the most forceful expressions in the New Testament. Look at verse 8. Why does it say, 'Remember Jesus Christ'? The context is the soldier, the athlete, the farmer and endurance. Listen to the words of Jesus in Matthew 10:22. Listen to the example of Jesus, supremely, in Hebrews 12:2. That's why Paul writes, 'Remember Jesus Christ.'

Then see Paul in verse 9, himself suffering for the gospel, 'wearing fetters like a criminal', yet enduring that suffering and despising the shame for the sake of Christ. It is this same Paul who wrote in Romans 5:3, 'We rejoice in our sufferings.' It is this same Paul who in 2 Corinthians 6:4 gives that great catalogue of ways of serving the Lord, beginning at the top of the list with – endurance.

The word means endurance in the heat and pain of suffering, for the gospel. Paul wouldn't have endured the suffering if he didn't believe that the gospel was supremely worth the cost. Nor would he have been content to be in prison if that had stopped the gospel. But look at verse 9 – one of the great sentences of the Bible – 'The word of God is not fettered.'

'The word of God is not fettered!' Shouted in Russia behind the Iron Curtain, across the annal of the darker days of China, in the tremendous grip of the Muslim states – that great truth is that which burns in Paul's heart that he's prepared to endure and despise the shame. This is why many of the Praetorian Guard were won to Christ by his witness, as he tells us in his epistle to the Philippians. Nothing can imprison the Word of God.

And he gives us this little couplet at the end, verses 11 to 13. There's a change of key, from major to minor; from 'If we have died with him . . .' to 'If we deny him . . .'

What does that mean? Well, perhaps it means that however much we fail, He alone knows the intent of our heart to serve. But William Hendriksen in his commentary suggests that the force of it is that He is faithful to His warnings as well as to His promises; that this God 'cannot deny himself'. And when we think of the parable of the foolish virgins or the unfaithful steward, we see that this is probably what it does mean.

So there is this serious contrast which we are to ponder on, and sing about, and realise, that endurance is one of the real qualities God wants. He wants every Christian to draw on the grace of Christ, to be committed, determined, working hard and ready to endure anything for the sake of the gospel, and for the Word of God that can never be fettered. May God make you and me those people, to His glory.

3. Ready for the Master's Use
(2 Timothy 2:14—3:13)

I want to look at four aspects of service that follow on from commitment, determination, hard work and endurance; four qualities that God wants in us, if we are to be ready and usable for Him.

Discernment of the truth (2:14–19)

Paul is concerned in these verses about people who play games with the faith. You and I who are concerned for the gospel of Christ are not in the business of playing games with it. It is a deadly serious business that calls for commitment and, particularly, discernment of the truth. As you look at these verses you will see that Paul is concerned about the way that Christians get upset, about the senseless controversies, about the way people hold the form of religion and deny its power, about counterfeit faith; and we are not to be people who play games like that in bringing the gospel to this fallen world. The quality that is needed is discernment.

The word isn't used here, but that is the force of the passage. It's what Paul prays for when he writes to the Philippians: 'that your love may abound more and more with . . . all discernment' (Phil. 1:9).

The lack of discernment in some Christians who are in most other ways excellent is, to my mind, both puzzling and astonishing. People who seem to be great Christians suddenly get caught up with some over-emphasis of an aspect of Christian truth, and their discernment goes out of the window. They follow the opinions of one group or another, and they are blown about by the latest fad or spiritual whizz-kid on the Christian trail, or the next Christian spectacular.

Now discernment over the truth and over secondary matters is what Paul is concerned with in this section of the epistle. I hope you will allow me to use a railway example.

Verse 14 is about *discerning what is an unprofitable branch line*. Branch lines are very important to the people who live on them, but nobody could ever say, for example, that the branch line from Windermere to Oxenholme up here in the Lake District is the most important piece of track in British Rail. Nobody would suggest that all British Rail's attention should be directed towards that line and the rest of British Rail be a mere ancillary to it. That would be absurd, but it is what tends to happen sometimes in Christian circles.

Look at verse 14. What is a branch line? 'Disputing about words.' The minutiae absorb totally disproportionate time and energy. Sometimes people judge all other Christians by whether or not they give importance and a particular interpretation to this branch line, that means more than anything else to them.

Some of the branch lines are advertised with all the flags out and great crowds are attracted to them; and there is razzmatazz, and brilliant communication, and a lot of money, a lot of publicity. And a lot of people are caught up into thinking that this is what really matters. That's why

Christians today need to have discernment, just as they did 2,000 years ago.

Paul charges us to avoid – that's the word, 'avoid' – and he says to us that if you go on with this it 'only ruins the hearers'. The word in the Greek is 'catastrophe' – that is the actual Greek word, *katastrophe*. It is catastrophic to a Christian to pursue the branch line as the thing that really matters above everything. Beware, my brothers and sisters; it is a trap around us in every direction in this country.

Secondly, however, verse 15 is about *discerning what is the main line of truth*. You can spend all your time rushing about, to contend with this heresy or that deviation, this over-emphasis, that branch line; but if you do that you are in danger of ignoring the main line itself to which God has committed us. Thus Timothy is reminded that he needs to be persistent in the main line of teaching. And I believe that is a message to many of us today, particularly those of us involved in teaching and in the ministry of the church. Beware, lest all the time you are fighting off everything else and ignoring the main lines of teaching.

People who go off into deviations and branch lines eventually long for the main line again. They come back hungry. And so we need churches all over the country which are persistent in the main line of teaching. Yes, contending with the errors; but not letting them dictate the programme. Do you accept this? It is an immensely important truth from the Word, and Timothy and we, and especially all of us involved in ministry, have to work and work at the Word, 'rightly handling the word of truth', in such a way as Paul says that God approves.

The word Paul uses means 'cutting a straight road'. Of course, that's what a railway does. Or you might notice a modern road coming to Keswick that cuts right through the hills. Now, what Paul is saying is that this is how you should handle the Word; you should cut a straight road. In a way that's what John the Baptist had to do when he had to prepare the way of the Lord; do you remember what the prophecy was? 'You will level the hills and fill the valleys.' In other words, you will prepare a straight clear road into which the Lord can come; and the preacher and the minister and the teacher and servant of the Word has to do that in the way in which he handles the Word.

It needs to be clear so that the Lord can move. It's an awesome responsibility. It's a responsibility that many of us involved in our early days, perhaps, of preaching, don't take seriously enough. It's only gradually that the awe of the pulpit, not the fear of man but the awe of God, of the deep responsibility of preaching or giving Bible readings or talking begin to dawn in on our souls, that this is something which in the end needs to be approved of God. This is why one has thought and re-thought and re-thought in this particular epistle that I am seeking to expound to you today.

For years, I never found speaking easy, because of my awe of God. And this drives us to dig and dig and compare and ponder and meditate and pray and plumb the amazing depths of the Word. Our task is to cut a straight road; the straight road of truth.

Thirdly (verses 16 to 18), it means *discerning what is a separate track altogether* – one not connected to the network at all. Paul describes these as 'godless chatter'. Godless, because it has nothing to do with the truth of God; chatter, because it's a load of verbiage, books, talks, discussions, TV, radio, newspaper and so forth pouring out. And (verse 16), it leads people into more and more ungodliness, further and further away from God and His holiness.

How necessary it is for young people to discern this, and any generation; but particularly those involved in universities and colleges and theological schools. I hope you are clear in your minds that there is an enormous amount of godlessness in theological schools! And anybody who seeks either to minister in a church, or to teach religious instruction or lead assembly in a school, or be a professor of theology, who doesn't know Christ is giving godless chatter – something which Paul is deeply concerned about, nineteen hundred years ago!

And it acts 'like gangrene' (verse 16), and today the media accelerate it because so often they love the outrageous. Godless drivel is given air time, it makes the headlines, it's news. And however much it spread like gangrene in Paul's day, it spreads like wildfire in our own. If I said something outrageous against God and the church on this platform this morning I guarantee you it would be on the one o'clock news! But nobody will report what I actually say (unless I have a slip of the tongue!). Truth isn't news.

In verses 17 and 18 we have Hymenaeus and Philetus, who were clearly leading members of the church. They taught that 'the resurrection is past already'. Paul had had to deal with this with the Corinthians (1 Cor. 15); and we find it about us today in things like *Godspell* and *Jesus Christ Superstar* – often with good content, but eliminating the resurrection.

It says of these two leaders that they had 'swerved from the truth', and yet they still seem to have been Christian leaders. And look at verse 18: 'They are upsetting the faith of some.' That is precisely what has concerned so many of us over recent months. How up-to-date the New Testament is! Or rather, how boringly repetitive heresy is.

You see how wonderfully relevant the Bible is. It's exciting, isn't it! I find it exciting – I hope you do – to open the Scriptures and find that they pound and pound and pound at the very world in which we live today, and yet they were written nearly two thousand years ago. What more evidence do you want of their inspiration?

So what do you do about it? You avoid it, says Paul. The best way to deal with heresy is to totally ignore it, to cut it off in a corner until it dies. It's difficult, because you feel that if you do that you are not contending with it, and so you are in the problem that the bigger publicity that heresy gets, the more it spreads its own gangrene. It's difficult. But wherever possible it's better to just let it be silent, and to be strong in your own faith so that you are not upset by the godless chattering, even of leading churchmen.

If you still need encouragement as you discern – discerning the branch line, the main line and the off-the-track errors which must be exposed and pushed aside, then come to verse 19. Be assured that 'God's firm foundation stands bearing this seal: "The Lord knows those who are his."' Amen! And no pronouncements or rulings or opinions or judgements, by ministers, theologians, bishops, moderators, or house church apostles will alter that fact.

The quote is of course from Numbers 16 and Korah's revolt against Moses and Aaron, and Moses' words to challenge the people. There were false teachers challenging the recognised ministry. But Paul reminds us that God is the arbiter. It is His church, and He knows who are His.

So the first aspect of being ready for the Master's use is discernment. God grant every one of us that, increasingly.

Holiness of life (2:20–23)

The second aspect of being ready for the Master's use is introduced at the end of verse 19, with the second quotation: 'Let every one who names the name of the Lord depart from iniquity.' A Christian who is committed, determined, hard-working and enduring, who is even discerning, but whose way of living is a disgrace to Christ in matters of morality or the fruit of the Spirit, or Christian grace, is of no use to the Master. Without love, as 1 Corinthians 13 puts it, we are nothing.

Take pride. How can God bless pride? A proud preacher – how can God bless his preaching? He'll only become more proud. How can God bless a proud organist or choir-master who only wants the applause of human beings, not of God? How can He bless a proud youth leader, or Sunday School teacher, or flower arranger? Where there is pride there may be some human sense of satisfaction, but God cannot bless it.

How can God use a person to spread the good news of the grace of Christ and of the transforming power of the Spirit if that person is dishonest at work, violent in temper, has an extra-marital relationship, or has an unbalancing love for him or her self? He can't. It would be to deny Himself.

Now, the picture here in verses 20 and 21 is of a great house, of the master of that house and of what is worthy of that master. Now understand as you ponder this (and I think you do need to stop and ponder it): 'What is this house?' That's question one, and the answer is, 'You are.' Then, 'Who is the master of this house?' Answer: 'Jesus Christ'. You and I are not our own, we are bought with a price. Christ, if we surrender to Him, enters the house of our life as master.

Let's take an illustration. Down the street, for many years, has been Fred's Fish Saloon. Its stained tables, greasy wallpaper and cracked lino have been there since the First World War. Then one day, to everybody's total surprise, there is a label across the window: 'Under new management'. The name changes. It becomes Frederick's Fish Restaurant. Fred is still there but he's no longer in charge. He's still employed there, but the quality of the business has changed.

Some of the nosey young people want to know what was going on, the day when the new manager-owner first went round the building. He looked at every part, including the parts the public weren't supposed to see. You could see him through the window pointing out to Fred the bits that ought to be changed. There was a sudden spring-clean. The old tables were thrown out, there was new wallpaper, there was more light – which immediately showed up more to be cleaned.

It was the same place, but it had undergone a transformation. So it is when Christ becomes master of the house of our life. He can only come as owner-manager. Across our life goes the label 'Under new management', and immediately He has to go everywhere. We may not want Him to, there may be parts of our life that we would love to have barred from His sight, but we know that nothing is outside His gaze. He immediately puts His finger on the things that need changing, and as He brings more light, so we see more that needs to be changed.

The cleaning process begins with a major spring-clean; or, to use Jesus' terminology in John 13, we first have a bath and then follows the constant foot-washing. So verse 21 is concerned with purifying. We are made clean by the Word (John 15), by confession of sin (1 John 1), by asking for washing and renewal (Psalm 51) – by action, by *doing* something about the things that we know are major offences to God. It is acting, and it is an on-going process. The Christian who has a sort of super-conversion and doesn't go in for foot-washing – constant purification – slides back. You and I know that we have to go on and on and on, spring-cleaning, cleaning, purifying, washing, wrestling with the inner nature which disgraces God.

See it spelt out further in verse 22: 'Shun youthful

passions.' Let me hasten to say that sexual relationship in the context of committed married love is a beautiful thing and a gift of God; but outside marriage it becomes a passion. 'Shun' is the word that means 'to run away'. I have talked with so many young people in my time at All Souls about this, and about the sort of parties that now happen all over the place, and they say, 'What does one do when things begin to deteriorate?'

The answer is, 'You get out!' And I point them to Joseph. What did he do? I know that the cost was prison, and misunderstanding, and accusation; but Joseph ran from the house when Potiphar's wife tried to trap him. There is a need to shun. We resist the devil, but we run away from youthful passions.

It's especially vital in ministers or leaders of the church. 1 Timothy 3:9 speaks about deacons as 'holding the mystery of the faith with a clear conscience', and that is vital. It's vital in every servant and youth leader and leader of the church. In one church I was in, there was a very good youth leader, but eventually, although he was serving the young people, the other side of his life was beginning to disgrace Christ. When one challenged him, he was not prepared to pay the price; and he's been in the wilderness now for the last twenty years.

Somebody pointed out to me after our last study, about that phrase in verse 13 about 'faithless he remains faithful' – he said 'I think that can be interpreted as saying that God simply goes round you if you are not faithful.' Certainly, that is true.

Then the positive, that which you run after, aiming at 'righteousness, faith, love, and peace' – and this marvellous sense that you find strength in seeing that you are not alone in aiming at those things: 'along with those who call upon the Lord from a pure heart.'

It is essential unless impossible, but essential wherever possible, that a Christian be in warm, understanding Christian fellowship. This is what stabilises people, particularly young people. If their total environment is among those who are not the Lord's, they are dragged and dragged. If you are called an 'oddball' because you are this or that as a Christian, it is when you come back to be with other Christians at places like Keswick that you are encouraged to realise that you are not alone. You are one of the very many people who run after the things of God.

All this, mercifully, is not in our own strength. The Holy Spirit not only exposes the wrong, but brings the fruit of the Spirit of love and joy and peace and so on. So go back to verse 21. We must want to be *holy*; do you want to be holy? Secondly we must want to be *consecrated* – that's the word used in the RSV – consecrated to Christ, to welcome Him as master of our life, in command of our life, whether that means being in the front line, in the public gaze, or in the back room – for Christ. Thirdly we must want to be *useful* to the Master. That's the word used here, 'useful'. Remember how Paul wrote to Philemon to receive back Onesimus? He had become a Christian, and now would become useful to Philemon because his motives would no longer be mixed. He wouldn't be someone who as a non-Christian was half serving his master and half serving himself; now, as a Christian, his motives would be clear and direct.

And this is true of us. Mixed motives in serving the Master are of no use, and our action and service in the church, the community and the world need to be clearly in obedience to the Master, as His hands and feet. And, fourthly, we must be *ready for any good work*, whenever and wherever it is.

Sensitivity in evangelism (2:23–26)

The third aspect of making us ready for the Master's use is really as much concerned with the people who have strayed onto the branch line or onto the off-beat lines, as with evangelism; but I want to keep both ideas in mind, because the truths are applicable to both.

In some senses, rescuing people from error is evangelism. Notice the titles you will need to have: firstly (verse 24) 'the Lord's servant'. If He is master of the house, then you are His servant; and as His servant, you have placed yourself under His command to serve Him. Secondly, you are to be a nurse. The little phrase 'kindly to every one' is only used elsewhere in 1 Thessalonians 2:7, where it says 'We were gentle among you, like a nurse taking care of her children.' It's a lovely picture of evangelism, or reaching the person astray. To be a nurse.

Now that means (verse 24) that you are not going to be 'quarrelsome', it means avoiding 'stupid, senseless controversies' (verse 23). It is very important that things that may matter – and actually matter quite a lot to us in our everyday Christian living – don't become the dominant issue. The nurse is concerned with the major issue, the chief priority of the person she cares for.

Let me give you the example of the woman who lived in our neighbourhood when we lived in the south of England. After many months she eventually plucked up the courage to go to church. She happened to be wearing trousers. Behind her, tragically, sat two stupid Christians, one of whom audibly said to the other, 'Fancy coming to church in trousers!' They destroyed the woman in six words.

That's not nursing, it's intolerable. It's an offence to the gospel. How can people be like it? When Christians are actually barriers to the faith, they are deadly. Pray God that

that is not true of anybody here. We need to be nurses, gentle, kindly, and this will mean going very carefully with people.

If a bottle of medicine is labelled 'one tablet per day', a nurse doesn't say 'Well, I'm going to speed up your recovery, take the whole lot.' But many naive evangelists do precisely that. They are hammering God-pills down the person's throat and the person hardly has time to take breath.

But watch a skilled evangelist. What happens? You'll see that person listening, trying to discern where the person is. That's the nurse. It's no use, if the patient complains of severe pain, prescribing two paracetamols if the person has appendicitis. And there is a great danger in not listening.

We are to be an 'apt teacher'. It's a quality required in a bishop; in 1 Timothy 3:2 it is the only special qualification besides a moral life, and I long that all ministers and all who teach in the Christian church should be trained as apt teachers. All of us who are involved in this need to be the best possible communicators of the truth, with illustration, application and so on. Apt teaching does not mean ten proof texts fired from a gospel repeater! It often means spending time with people over a period of months, helping them to see and understand and think through what is involved.

Then we must be 'forbearing' towards opponents, just as God is forbearing to us (Romans 2:4). I remember a man coming to All Souls who'd been to the Festival of Light rally a few weeks previously. He'd gone to criticise the Christians, but the one thing that had cracked his armour was that fact that while he and all the atheists were throwing vileness at the Christians, they loved him in return. It was amazing, it cracked his armour, and in God's mercy he came to Christ.

You don't win people by violent reaction or by pillorying

them, you win them by forbearance, love, and 'correcting' your 'opponents, with gentleness'. Oh, learn this! The false teachers of 2 Timothy 2 are won back to the truth by love and care, not by condemnation or confrontation; and it's true in personal evangelism. In the 'Agnostics Anonymous' groups run at All Souls, you are able to bring your agnostic friend for the first week, but then you are banned as a Christian from that group. That is to stop the stupid things that often happen in Christian circles when some enquirer finally manages to ask a question, and is cut down by someone in the group who says 'Don't you know Hezekiah 3:6?'!

All this, to share in God's work. Look at the last verse. If God brings them to faith, He will stand guard over them. So we prepare the way; the teaching, loving, nursing, so that God in His mercy may perhaps 'grant that they will repent' – change their mind – so that they will come back to the truth, the orthodox faith which Paul means here.

'And they may escape from the snare of the devil' – the idea is that of becoming sober after being drunk or drugged. You know, the world does this to people; its ways of thinking, its standards, can act like a drug until they are ensnared in the devil's net. False ways of thinking about God's truth can appear more exhilarating than orthodox faith, and it dulls our discernment and we are captured by the devil.

But the one thing that slays the devil is the Word of God, and this passage urges us in evangelism to approach those in error; to seek to explain the truth with patience, gentleness, skill and love; to pray for the miracle of God's action to bring them out of the devil's captivity into the liberty of the children of God.

Understanding of worldliness (3:1–9)

Very briefly, my last point. It's actually very difficult to expound it.

Here we read of the effects of a godless society, the breakdown of normal relationships between people, 'times of stress' (verse 1). Every generation of Christians has applied this passage to themselves, 'times' is plural. And it's true today.

'Lovers of self, lovers of money' – look at the way some of our multiples are hell-bent on Sunday opening. Family life warped, disobedience to parents, ingratitude, unholiness, inhumanity, implacability – that means, never forgiving.

In the church, verses 4 and 5, 'lovers of pleasure rather than lovers of God' – God fitted in, but not as Lord. 'Holding the form of religion but denying the power of it' – it's a terrible thing, nominal Christianity. Or verses 6 and 7; a bunch of weak women idolising an influential person in the church but never having their lives changed or accepting the truth for themselves. Or verse 8; corrupted minds and counterfeit faith.

Paul says, 'Don't get het up about it, it's been like it from the beginning' (verse 13). So understand it, don't get rattled. It will go on; so don't misunderstand what the world is like and worldliness in the church is like, but meet it by unswerving commitment to the teaching and living truth, just as in chapter 2 verse 15.

So in verses 10–12 learn from Paul that he met the world not by running after every false trail, but by teaching, conduct, aim in life, faith, patience, love and steadfastness with persecutions and sufferings as inevitable in the life of God. He ploughed a straight furrow, cut a clear road, kept to the triumph; and whatever the attacks of the world swirling around us, the gospel of Christ is for ever, and His kingdom and His family are for ever.

May this encourage every Christian, and may God grant

us the qualities of discernment of truth, holiness of life, sensitivity in evangelism and understanding of worldliness so that we may be equipped, ready for the Master's use.

4. Equipped for Every Good Work (2 Timothy 3:14—4:22)

After all the problems of the side-tracks and the godless chatter and worldliness in society and the church, Timothy is turned back to Scripture; and it's like coming home. Scripture is security, comfort, good food to the soul, cleansing – it's familiar ground, and how good it has been to share that Word here. Despite all the theological wildness in our country and in the church, all the various doubts and denials and deviations and drivel, we can come back to Scripture and it's marvellous! Secure like a rock in a storm, like light in the darkness, like pure air instead of pollution, like sunshine instead of rain.

So, Timothy, says Paul, understand the worldliness, avoid the stupid controversies, imposters will go from bad to worse; but as for you (verse 14), stand on Scripture. That's the force of the closing part of this epistle.

There are at least three aspects of the Scriptures that are emphasised here, that I want to outline to you.

Constancy in the Scriptures (3:14–15)

In verse 14 the word 'continue' means settling in permanently. It's the word you use when you arrive where you're now going to live, where you're going to unpack. I think the context suggests that Timothy may have been rocked a bit by the swirling influences around, affecting his faith – as many people are being rocked in this present day.

When I was studying for my divinity degree, I was rocked in this way. I had been brought to Christ in an evangelical church, and I hadn't been introduced to much of the critical approach to the Bible. What rocked me was the feeling that evangelicals did not have the answer; and I began to move from one foot to the other over Scripture.

I was thankful to those who helped me back. There were different factors that God used in His mercy. One, strangely enough, was a sermon on the devil; partly in the way that the person expounded Scripture and made me realise that the theories of the devil as a sort of symbol of evil simply don't work when you look at Scripture and understand it. Another was doing a Bible Study on Genesis 3.

But I am thankful to God for one of His saints who I think is now with Him; H.G. Ellison. It was his teaching from the Old Testament that brought me back to the rock of Scripture, because Ellison was prepared to expound the critical position to the last iota, until you thought that only Houdini could get out of it; and then he would say in his inimitable way – 'But!'

Then he took it apart, and showed me that what looked incredibly significant actually fell apart when you looked at it. I am thankful to Ellison because it was through him that I came back to Scripture as God's Word and settled in – permanently.

That is what Paul is saying to Timothy. 'You've been through it, you've been rocked, now settle down.' And any of you who are off balance due to theological meanderings at university or college, or caught up in the novelty of something new, I want to urge you that if God has shown you at Keswick afresh the dynamite of His Word, that you will come home and settle in permanently to Scripture for the rest of your life.

That is what Timothy is urged to do. It was coming home, because that was how he had been brought up. Look first at verse 15: there had been *acquaintance* 'with the sacred writings' – that's more than Scripture, but especially Scripture – from childhood.

What does 'acquaintance' mean? It's a getting-to-know-you exercise. It's getting to know the family. It's taking the children round the family portrait gallery, introducing them to Great-Grandad Abraham, Grandma Sarah, Uncle Moses, Auntie Esther, Uncle Paul and all the many thousands and millions of those who make up the family of the Lord. That's why in my youth it was reading short Christian biographies that had the greatest effect on me. And it is acquaintance with the family that is where children need to begin.

Secondly, after acquaintance comes '*instruction* for salvation'. In the church at All Souls we fought strongly for the policy and idea of being a church family. I've always so fought in my own ministry. But a child that grows up in a Christian environment is in the family, but has to come to a point when he consciously becomes a member of the family by his own conviction. It may be conversion, though it is not necessarily so, but it is certainly the moment when they make it their own. They may be very young. Our own daughter came to the point of faith at six, and it was confirmed later on.

Because of this, the handling of Scripture with them is so important in the home or Sunday School or junior church. I hope you assign great importance to the care of children in your church family. Wouldn't you protest if your eight-year old was being taught in primary school by a fourteen-year old? Yet this is what we do in many of our Sunday Schools. There should be an open budget for anything to do with communication and facilities. When I find some Sunday Schools using pictures produced thirty years ago, I wonder just what on earth they think they are doing in today's world.

I want to underline that the handling of Scripture with children is of the greatest importance, and we should commit it only to those who are trained in method and content, and we should go on retraining. And of course though this is true for children, it is true for anybody – that the Scriptures, as Paul says to Timothy, are the key to salvation. Remember John 20:31 – 'these are written that you may believe . . .'

A little while ago, in a mission in my own diocese, I made a challenge which is a custom of mine to make in most evangelistic services. I challenged the audience that if they were honestly seeking, they should pray 'God, if you exist, open yourself to me through your Word', and then, meaning it, begin to read John's Gospel. I have found over the years that it is seldom later than John 7 before they come to faith. A few weeks ago we were in a church in the diocese and met a woman from that meeting who'd done just that – I think she got to John 6 – and was now radiating the faith. Simply through the Scriptures.

John says that that's what the Gospel is there for. This is why in personal evangelism you need to open the Bible and get them to look at the text. And it is why Scripture distribution is so important.

I don't have to spell it out to you. The salvation is, in the end of course, by faith; but the instruction for it is through Scripture.

Thirdly, in verse 14 – going back a bit – there is '*continuing* in what you have learned'. Again, you remember, this is the pattern, the architect's sketch, the non-negotiable truths of the Christian faith. After salvation we need to nurse people immediately on to the main factors of the faith, so that they may grasp them, understand them, begin to live by them and grow with them by the power of the Holy Spirit.

Fourthly, Paul speaks of *firmly believing*. This is a parallel stage; not just a faith about salvation, but a trusting God as God. That is a very big step to take. The last thing that some churches will do is to get on their knees.

And this is the force of it, it's those first early steps – do you remember them, when you first came to Christ? Those first early steps of actually beginning to trust the promises of God in His Word, tremulously, but gradually taking a few steps and finding that God is honouring His Word. We begin to walk, and then to run. But it is that first step of taking faith like that, in prayer, in drawing on the resources of God to serve and to speak and to witness.

This is why sometimes corporate acts of faith in the church are such a help. Faith projects such as building programmes can often be a great release for people. The rebuilding of All Souls did that for a large number of people, not least in taking the step as a church with much prayer and thought, believing that this was the only thing we could do and that God was leading us into it.

But there was also detail on the way; God did a great many remarkable things for us, and when God does such things, people in the congregation think 'Wow!' And, again, they take the first faltering steps for themselves, so that at the end of the project most of us who were involved in it could never be the same again. God was in it, and it was a project of faith.

This is 'firmly believing'. It is not simply a matter of believing in your mind, but taking steps of trust in God out of the Scriptures.

It is helped by the lives of those who taught us – 'knowing from whom you learned it' (verse 14). Timothy could look at Paul not only as a teacher of the truth but as a demonstrator of that truth in his own life. There can be no doubting Paul's faith, a glowing testimony of his life, commitment, love, worship and joy.

My brothers and sisters: can young people look to us and find the faith attractive? Can they look to us and see us working it through, with a testimony of commitment and love and worship and joy? Are they inspired by you?

It's a great tragedy, when churches have some cantankerous old people amongst them who are a disgrace to the gospel. It is a most damaging thing to young people, not to be able to see the senior Christians in the church aglow with Christ. The greatest contribution any older Christian can make is to be a glowing example to the young people.

So there are the stages. Acquaintance, salvation, learning, trusting, believing, the help and example of fine Christians. And all this enables us to weather the swirling storms of doubts and attacks on Scripture, so that even if we temporarily lose our footing, eventually we settle down permanently to the Scriptures as our authority in life.

Completion by the Scriptures (3:16–17)

'Complete' is a little word that comes at the end of verse 17. This is one of the most important texts of the New Testament, and I am going to try to spell it out in some detail.

All the words in the verse are important. Firstly, the word for Scripture is 'writings', which was always, in the New Testament, equivalent to the Old Testament. We extend it in our thinking to the New Testament, because of the way that the New Testament was formed – not as an inspired collection of writings, but as a collection of inspired writings. The early church recognised them as standing out from others, as having apostolic authority, and so the New Testament canon was formed.

Already there are clues in the New Testament itself. In 2 Peter 3:16, for example, Peter speaks about Paul's writings as Scripture. Already they are being so regarded. Paul speaks as using words taught by the Spirit. He gives orders for his letters to be read in churches, which is what you did in the Old Testament. So I think it is quite right for us to take this description of Scripture in verse 16 and include in it the New Testament.

If you have an RSV you'll notice that in the margin it says, 'Every scripture inspired of God is profitable.' That's how the NEB translates it, too. Now which is right? Because there is a world of difference. If 'every scripture inspired of God is profitable', then you are wide open to the question, 'Which bits are inspired?' It becomes a subjective thing, or a balancing of scholarly votes, or an acceptance that there is no certainty about anything in the New Testament. You're wide open.

So what does the Greek actually say? 'All', 'Scripture' ('the writings'), 'inspired by God' (one word in the Greek, 'God-breathed') – and then follows the most important word, that you need to get hold of: '*and*'. Now – follow the RSV margin or the NEB. 'Every scripture inspired of God is profitable for . . .' – but where's the 'and'? It's not there. But you can't translate it like that with the 'and' in. That word forces you to the translation that you have 'All Scripture is inspired by God and . . .'

Even the most liberal of scholars will admit that this is the correct translation. You can say 'Every scripture' – indeed, that's quite likely the correct translation, and it contends against those who want to pick and choose in the Scriptures like a shopper in the market place. But you must have the 'and'. It is very important that we stand on that truth.

'Inspired' means 'God-breathed' – through the personalities and characters of people, the poets, the historians, the prophets, the psalmists. But the emphasis is that God is the initiator; Scripture is from the mind of God by His Spirit in His words. 'The heart of God is in the words of God,' said Gregory the Great, Bishop of Rome in 684.

But however much the truth of the scriptural word here which I have spelt out to you, it is the experience of the Scriptures that can mean so much more. In the end, for me, it's not the arguments or the theories that really prove the point, it's the Scriptures themselves. Though it's important to understand the facts as we have been trying to handle them, it is a fact that this Word is constantly an inspiration to one's soul.

That is for me, and I trust for you, the confirming fact that this is the Word of God. You can turn back again and again to His Word and find God speaking to you through it. And when some of the present opponents are saying publicly, 'The only thing that matters to us is the experience of Christ, not the Scriptures,' I say back to them, 'You are discounting all of us who experience God in the Scriptures.' That is just as valid an experience.

So it is in the way in which the Word opens up to us that we are confirmed in our hearts about its inspiration. Many of you are old enough to remember the first translation that most of us used, that of J.B. Phillips – *Letters to Young Churches*. Phillips was not an evangelical. He had no approach to the Bible as being the Word of God. He simply approached it as a translator.

At the time of the *Honest to God* controversy, a clergyman hung himself because he thought that all he had taught over the years had been wrong. Phillips was so angry, that he wrote a book called *Ring of Truth*. In it he testified that in the translating of the Bible 'hand-to-hand', its power had overwhelmed him. Later he said, 'Translating the New Testament was like rewiring a house with the mains left on.' What better testimony could you have? It should be shouted from the housetops at the present time.

Now it is this confidence that Scripture is God-breathed that makes it the means of completely equipping the Christian. It could not be so if it were not inspired, or inspired in part. It also means that we cannot mess about with Scripture. As long ago as 1835, J.H. Newman described rationalism as 'speaking of the revelation of God as the Word of God, and treating it as the word of man . . .' It's still the same, 150 years later. That is what people do to the Scriptures, and we must stand back and say, 'But they are God-breathed, and you cannot mess around with them like that.' They are the equipment for the Christian.

Equipment in four ways. Profitable, as you see, for *teaching*. Expository teaching is vital in our churches. If you don't get it – demand it! For *study*; study in groups is the basis of our authority, teaching, teaching, teaching the Word. Profitable for *reproof*, for showing us what is wrong, for exposing things; so that is often a very uncomfortable word for us. And for *correction*. It means 'lifting a person back on his feet', restoring him to a true way of living.

'Training in righteousness' is being made to be like Christ, conforming to His will and His way in every aspect of life. 'That the man of God' – particularly the minister, the preacher, the leader, but also any Christian – 'may be equipped'; and it is only as we grow in the Scriptures and obey and learn and respond, that we can be truly complete and equipped for the ministry of Christ.

The Bible is God's gift to us. Roy Clements has reminded us that Jesus never took a pen, but that the Holy Spirit was entrusted with bringing the truth to the apostles and through them to you and to me.

At the beginning of the century, Bishop Handley Moule, then Bishop of Durham, wrote a commentary on 2 Timothy. He began with these words. Listen to them as from a bishop of Durham. 'Personal attention to the very words of Holy Scripture, in the spirit of obedience and prayer, was never more needed in the Christian church than now.' Amen.

Commission with the Scriptures (4:1–22)

Now we move into chapter 4. Paul hands Timothy a commission, just as I do to clergy who stand or kneel before me at their ordination. In the Church of England, when we ordain deacons the only thing we give them – and priests, and bishops – is the Bible. We hand it to them publicly. To the deacon we say, 'Receive this book as the sign of the authority given you this day to speak God's Word to His people; build them up in His truth and serve them in His name.' To the bishops: 'Receive this book, here are the words of eternal life; take them for your guide and declare them to the world.' That's the commission laid upon all bishops, whether they fulfil it or not.

And so Paul says to Timothy, 'I charge you.' It is his last will and testament and command.

Note what is in it and what is not in it. Signs and wonders are not mentioned in this epistle. They are not Paul's major concern at all in his last testament to the church. His major concern is the gospel. As you stand with him in his prison cell, I think you get your priorities right. It is not just to Paul to whom Timothy must answer, any more than it is to a bishop a clergyman must answer, but all of us are going to answer to the Lord.

So this charge is in the presence of God and Christ Jesus. We are all of us going to be answerable not to man, but 'to Christ who is to judge the living and the dead.' 'By his appearing' reminds us of the talents and the stewards and the foolish virgin parables, and His kingdom, His reign, and His lordship. So it is Jesus as judge and Lord and king to whom I shall hand back my bishopric, to whom you will hand back your ministry, whatever it is, in the church.

Then come the details of the commission, in verse 2. 'Preach the Word.' You needed to hear it, Timothy; you have been commanded to follow it, to guard it, to learn it, to teach it to others, and now – to preach it. To the world, the folly of preaching; but God's truth, and God's way. 'Be urgent in season and out of season' – don't desert your post if the going gets tough, don't just preach if you feel like it.

There needs to be courage over this. Sometimes I get letters from clergymen seeking livings in my diocese. I write back and ask them to say more about themselves, and they write back: 'I would like to go to a parish where my preaching will be appreciated.' My heart drops. What about the hundreds of churches where people have never learned to be responsive to teaching? Who's going to go there? Who's going to suffer, perhaps even to be crucified in one way or another by the congregation, yet lay the ground perhaps for the next man to be able to minister the Word? Where are the pioneers?

We are committed to be in season and out of season. That is, whether it's welcome or whether we seem to be preaching to a brick wall.

We are to 'convince', that is, learn how to argue the gospel, to teach it and explain it rather than just shout it aloud. We need to 'rebuke' – the comfort and discomfort of the

Word of God! – to 'exhort', that is, the appeal to conversion and consecration – and we are to 'be unfailing in teaching and patience'. Not pushy, but steadily expounding the Word.

All this, in the negative atmosphere of verses 3 and 4. There are people who will not endure sound teaching. When we were working in Manchester, somebody actually complained to me that the preaching was too personal! What a description of today is Paul's marvellous phrase, people who have 'itchy ears'. I'm afraid it's within the church. Always wanting something new, something to tickle their ears.

Meeting many people in the secular world, which I do as a bishop, I find that many of the 'high-up' people in our land are totally awash over the Truth. It's a strange world we are in. Think of the influence of that stupid book, *Chariots of the Gods*. It sold millions of copies. Today in the consciousness of many young people, God is an astronaut. The book did enormous damage. It was filmed, and the film was distributed with *The Railway Children*, which many children went to see.

Satan is very clever. We're awash with the 'itching ears' complex outside and inside the church, and people are turned away from the truth and led into myths. It's in the midst of this that all who love Christ and believe His Word is truth need to preach, and teach, in season and out.

The summary (4:5–22)
We stand again in the prison cell. We look at Paul in his fetters about to be martyred for the gospel. Having poured out his last words to Timothy and to you and me and the church of God, he now sums up in a four-point charter. Take it as your own, as we end this epistle.

Always be steady. Will you do that with me? Don't lose

your nerve. Don't be blown away by every new fad or branch-line. Keep on the main line, with Christ at the centre. *Enduring suffering.* The great theme of chapters 1 and 2. Suffering is inevitable for the servant of God, and if Timothy is afraid of that then he must get over it and know that God has given him the spirit of love and power and self-control. Are you prepared to endure suffering? Thirdly, *Do the work of an evangelist* – the main driving task of every Christian and the church. The gospel is our central task. Fourthly, *Fulfil your ministry*, whatever it is you're called to be. The task God has given you is to be seen through to the end. It is God's task entrusted to you, you are equipped by Him to fulfil it, and He expects you to set your hand to that plough and not to look back. Don't lose your steam in later years! So here is the great charge to us.

And then comes the great farewell. Paul sees himself as a sacrifice, a libation (verse 6) to his Lord. 'The time of my departure has come' – the word used is *analusis*, 'setting free'. It's the word for when a boat leaves harbour. For Paul it's not a reluctant, but a purposeful departure. He's packed, ready to go, looking forward to all that lies ahead.

The three pictures in verse 7 are from chapter 2. The retiring soldier – 'I have fought the good fight.' The retiring athlete – 'I have finished the race.' The retiring farmer – 'I have kept the faith' (which means literally, 'gone on', like a farmer fulfilling a farming task).

All that he had enjoined upon Timothy is evidenced in this marvellous life of Paul's. Jesus ran the race before Him; He endured the cross and despised the shame. Now Paul has run the race, he has endured, he has despised the shame, even the fetters on his legs as this letter was being written. Now the joy was set before him, the garland of the 'Well-done!', given to God's righteous servant by the righteous judge.

In this, his last will and testament, Paul has done everything to encourage Timothy and you and me to run that race in the same way. His letter inspired by the Holy Spirit has been given to inspire us to run the race set before us just as he did.

People will come and go. There will be Demases (verse 10) who love this present world. There will be people like faithful Luke, practical Mark, evil Alexander. There will be practical needs – clothing, books; times of living simply, tough times (verse 17). There will be love and encouragement from various Christian families, and there will be those like Trophimus (verse 20) who will fall ill (notice, Paul was unable to heal him).

But the main thrust to us today is that we might commit and recommit ourselves afresh to the Lord, with the one life He has given us to live for Him, and to concentrate on the main line of the faith with the centrality of the gospel. Becoming better and better equipped, with all that that means in the wider significance of the community as well as the church; cleansed; trained; committed; so that every man and woman in the church, old or young, by God's mercy might say at the end of their lives, 'I have fought the good fight, I have finished the race, I have kept the faith.' So that every one of us might live as those 'chained to the gospel', for the sake of the Lord of that gospel.

And what more can I add, than what Paul adds as his final word to Timothy and to the church before his death? 'The Lord be with your spirit. Grace be with you.'

THE ADDRESSES

THE SOWER

by Rev Eric Alexander

Luke 8:4–21

I want to ask you to turn with me to the first half of Luke 8, which was our reading. It has a single theme and it is the theme which, in my judgement, most urgently confronts us at the beginning of every Convention here at Keswick; the theme of the cardinal importance of a right hearing of the Word of God.

It's Jesus' repeated theme, you will notice. In the parable of the sower, He cries out in verse 8 'He who has ears to hear, let him hear'; and He does not just say it, He calls out, or cries out. And then in the parable of the lamp, from verses 16–18, the lamp that was lit to be set on a stand, rather than hidden under a bed of course; again Jesus presses this issue. Verse 18: 'Take heed then how you hear.' And then in the whole issue of who is most closely related to Jesus, in verses 19–21, where they came to Him and said to Him that in the midst of this crowded situation, His mother and brothers were earnestly wanting to press in upon Him. Jesus says, in verse 21, 'My mother and my brothers are those who hear the word of God and do it.'

It's obvious that in Jesus' judgement, almost everything turns upon this issue of the right hearing of the Word of

God.

You will notice that He is not speaking about those who have never heard, nor is He speaking about those who choose not to hear. He is speaking about people like ourselves who hear the Word, and whatever else happens this week at Keswick, we are going to be in the presence of the Word of God, and subject to a fair diet of God's Word – we are going to be hearers of the Word in some sense, but from what Jesus says, you will see that so many things depend upon how we hear. The crucial issue is that we take heed how we hear God's Word.

Jesus says, for example, that our eternal destiny depends upon it, in verse 12. If we hear in such a way that our hearts are 'hard ground' and the devil snatches the Word away, we shall not be saved. More than that, our spiritual well-being depends upon it (verse 18). It is this whole issue of our right hearing of the Word of God that will determine whether we are going to be spiritually enriched at the end of this week, or impoverished and left desolate.

That which we think we have – will be taken from us. An immensely serious responsibility rests upon us. We are hearing the Word of God, and again our relationship with Christ depends upon it (verse 21). Jesus says that a relationship with Him is not an external or outward mechanical matter, it is conditioned upon our hearing and obeying the Word of God.

Now you may be here this week and feel that there is a certain coldness in your heart. Maybe that's why you have come again and again – because you have a sense of distance in your soul, between yourself and God. There is something inside hollow and lacking. How is that dealt with?

Well, our Lord says, the key to a new intimacy is a right hearing of the Word of God, and a true obedience to it. Let me spell out for you the three propositions that Jesus here puts before us in these paragraphs, and then try to unfold them a little.

It is possible to hear the Word of God unprofitably (verses 4–15)

That's the general teaching and theme of the parable of the sower; at least, in the first three sections. And it's about this that Jesus had most to say.

There are two warnings that Jesus gives us in the Gospels about hearing the Word of God. One is this: 'Take heed what you hear' (Mark 4:24). The other is here in Luke 8:18. 'Take heed how you hear.' The first is a warning about the need to examine the truthfulness of the teaching to which we submit ourselves. That is, our lives are not simply to be open fields for any kind of sowing, we are to be discerning about what we hear. But the second warning is to examine ourselves and the condition of our hearts as we hear. It assumes the truthfulness of the teaching. The seed is the good seed of the Word that Jesus is speaking about, but the warning is 'Take heed to the condition of your hearts as you receive the Word of God.'

Now there are some of us who find it very easy to take heed to the first warning. We would be anxious to avoid ministry that was not faithful to the Word of God. But it's very easy for us to escape the second warning, my brothers and sisters, and never really to be concerned about the condition of our hearts as we come to hear the Word of God. And it makes us ask 'What kind of ground is my heart, as the seed of God's Word is sown into it this week?'

I wouldn't be at all surprised if there are some of us here at Keswick this evening, and deep down perhaps, we have rationalised it. We would not articulate it in this way, but there are certain things about which we are determined God will not speak to us or teach us this week. And I say to you, are you here with a teachable spirit? Because that's what the open heart reveres.

Notice the three warnings that Jesus gives us in this parable. Warning one is in verses 5 and 12; 5 is the parable, 12 is the interpretation of it which we have from the lips of Jesus, so we don't need to speculate. He spells it out for us line by line, and warns us that it is possible to hear the Word of God with clarity, but without faith and without experiencing salvation.

Listen to what Jesus says (verse 12). 'The ones along the path are those who have heard, then the devil comes and takes away the word from their hearts that they may not believe and be saved.' Now that's a simple matter of fact.

The Word of God is living and powerful and contains within it the seed germ of eternal life and of a new creation. Says Peter 'You have been born anew. Not of perishable seed, but of imperishable through the living and abiding word of God.' But I want to say to you this evening, the power and effectiveness of the Word of God does not operate mechanically, automatically or inevitably. And if your heart is, for some reason, hardened towards God, like a well-trodden path, however true the Word of God is that you hear, the devil will delight to come and snatch it away. He will cooperate with the hardness of your heart and prevent you from believing.

However the hardness may have been produced and whatever the guise it may wear, let me say to you this evening, that there are hearts which are conservative, evangelical, orthodox and everything else, and as hard as flint. Whatever the origin or the form that the hardness takes, it is a desperately serious disease.

Now the question is, how do you deal with a hard heart? Well, the answer is that only God can change a heart of stone into a heart of flesh. The amazing thing is, that this is precisely what He promises to do. 'I will give to you a new heart and a new spirit I will put within you. And I will take out of your flesh the heart of stone, and I will give you a heart of flesh. And I will put my spirit within you and cause you to walk in my statutes and to observe my ordinances' (Ezek. 36:26). We need to cry to God, 'Oh God, take away this hard heart in my spirit and give me a heart of flesh! Put your spirit within me and set your laws in my heart.'

Warning number two: it is possible to hear the Word of God with superficial acceptance but without eternal life. That's the point of the seed which fell on rocky soil (verse 13). In some ways it is the opposite problem. There is an immediate glad, willing response. There is an excitement almost, about hearing the Word of God, and an immediacy about the response to it. But the real issue is not, 'Have I received it warmly and joyfully? Have I been enthusiastic in embracing it?' The real issue is, 'How deep has it gone?'

There are several forms that this shallowness takes. It can be a shallow emotionalism, but it can also be a shallow intellectualism. There are many students who have this problem; they're absorbed with a merely intellectual interest in the truth of God. But God does not deal with intellectual dilettantes.

We are made up not just of emotion and intellect, but also of will. And it's when the Word of God goes down to grip our wills and lay hold of the citadel of self – that's the time when the Word of God has penetrated through the rock and has gripped us where it really matters. But it is possible to have a shallow response to the Word of God.

Warning number three (verses 7 and 14). It is possible to hear the Word of God with interest, but without repentance. That's the message of the seed falling among thorns. It is the Word of God accommodated in an unchanged life (verse 14). And the result is, of course, that the real energies of the soil are not devoted to the maturing and growing of the seed; they are devoted to something else altogether. And it's possible for us to be here this week at Keswick, and not really to have this issue clear – I mean clear in our own soul. It is possible – proposition one – to hear the Word of God unprofitably.

Now, more briefly proposition two.

It is possible to hide the Word of God dangerously (verses 16–18)

These verses are a little parable. It seems that what Jesus is referring to is the Word of God which is like a lamp; and Scripture speaks of itself as a light.

The theme is that there is a right and a wrong way to hide the Word of God. The Psalmist tells us in Psalm 119:11 that he has hidden the Word of God in his heart, that he might not sin against Him. But this parable is about hearing and knowing God's Word, and then hiding it and burying it lest it disturb us and challenge the darkness. For there are certain words from God that He speaks to us that we are inclined to hide away, because they are uncomfortable to us. And that's dangerous in two ways:

IT'S DANGEROUS FOR OTHERS: In verse 16, Jesus is clearly telling us that others are affected by our hiding the Word. If it shines like a light and is displayed, those who enter the house are drawn by the light into the house. And Jesus is clearly speaking of those who are outside of the kingdom of His grace. The light, when it shines as a lamp is intended to shine, leads and draws others into the house. It shows them the way, but if it is hidden, they are left in darkness and caused to stumble.

There's clearly a missionary note in what Jesus is saying. I would not at all be surprised if this refers to the Jews who were given the revelation of God in Holy Scripture. And they were given it in order that they might be a light to lighten the Gentiles, that the Gentiles might come to His light. But instead of displaying it, the Jews hid it and the Gentiles were left in darkness.

My dear friends, if we do not rightly hear the Word of God, others will be affected by it, and we will be responsible for them. Your right hearing of the Word of God is going to affect the lives of other people, and you'll be responsible for them before God. Jesus says 'After a lamp is lit and is put on a stand, those who enter see the light.' It is not hidden away. But *it's dangerous also for ourselves*, to hide the light.

Jesus comes to the climax of this parable in verse 18. 'Take heed therefore, how you hear' – it's dangerous for ourselves. Verse 17 tells us, 'Nothing is hid that shall not be made manifest, nor anything secret that shall not be known and come to light'. In other words, God is going to uncover and expose all that He has taught us, all that we have heard. This is the responsibility of hearing the Word of God.

One day, God is going to expose it before us, and hold us accountable for it. And I believe this is what Jesus is speaking about here. The language is the language of judgement, and He will bring it all out one day, and say, 'Now you did have the privilege of hearing that, did you not? You did know the truth, did you not? It was not that you didn't know it; that Word was sown on the ground of your heart.' And it will be a solemn day when God comes to confront us with that, with the privileges of what we hear. God is going to hold us responsible, Beloved, for this.

In verse 18 we see that a wrong hearing of the Word of

God exposes us to spiritual poverty. When we hide the Word of God in this wrong sense, so often we discover that the very area of the ministry of God's Word that we will want to retain, God has taken from us; because disobedience displeases Him.

It is possible to heed the Word of God fruitfully (verses 15–21)

This, of course, is the message of the fourth area in which the seed is sown.

The idea in verse 15 of 'heeding' is defined for us by Jesus as 'holding fast the word'; and that really is the reverse of all superficial dealing with God's Word. It is allied at the end of verse 15, with the word for perseverance in the New Testament – 'He who holds fast the word of God in an honest and good heart and will bring forth fruit with perseverance.'

Now it is that which is a right hearing, a true heeding of the Word of God, but it's spelled out for us in a different way, in verse 21.

The whole issue in this incident, of Jesus' mother and brothers is the issue of access to Jesus and intimacy with Him. They're standing outside. They say, 'We want to come in and speak with Him, because we have a special relationship with Him.' But Jesus says, 'The only thing that ultimately matters to Me, the only relationship that ultimately tells with Me, is the one I have with those who hear the Word of God and obey it.'

There is no status in the Christian world. There is no position that any of us has ever held, there is no reputation that you may have in any sphere, that will be of the slightest interest to God. The only thing that really matters to Him is the hearing and obeying of His Word. Those who hear and obey are those who have found the secret of intimacy with Jesus, and the fruit in their lives is immeasurable.

WITH GOD IN THE VALLEY

by Rev Donald Bridge

Genesis 32:22–32

The brook Jabbok which we are going to read about is not the placid babbling stream that the English word 'brook' in the Authorised Version suggests. It flings itself down from the purple mountains of Moab. Much of the year it is a dry water-course, like most of the rivers there, cutting deep into the steep mountain slope, dropping and twisting and plunging, its high cliff shutting out the sun a good deal of the time. When it occasionally rains, the whole place becomes a roaring torrent of rapids and waterfalls, sweeping away rocks and trees, undermining the banks, throwing boulders across the road that fords it, tearing and splitting the modern tarmac where the river runs across the road.

This is the situation you have in Genesis 32:22–27. We'll leave it at verse 27 for the moment. It is a very dramatic story: an earlier generation knew it as the story of 'Wrestling Jacob'. Wesley's great hymn/poem was based on it – 'Come O Thou Traveller Unknown'. It is actually the story of a believer in God who got around after rather too long to facing himself and what he was.

It may be that when I say that it is what we are going to talk about for a while – looking at ourselves and facing up to what we are in the sight of God – that some of you may well feel, 'How irrelevant can you get? How inward-looking can you get, in a world of terrorism and high-jacking, in a world where one pop concert can reach 80 percent of the world's television-watching population, in a world where famine on a scale of global catastrophe faces us – whatever are you doing? Could anything possibly be more irrelevant than to urge five thousand people to look inside at themselves?'

But you know, all of those problems, all of those situations that I gave just quickly quoted almost at random from the world's headlines pose the question, 'Who am I, what am I?' or, in the words of Psalm 8, 'What is man?'

This story tells us of Jacob's self-discovery and directs us on a course of self-discovery which is totally relevant to the state of the world and the problems we face, because the world is in the state it is in because it consists of human nature.

There is a tremendously striking contrast in this story to what is beginning to be called the 'gospel of success', that some Christians are preaching on American television. It could be summed up in the phrase: 'Our biggest problem is our lack of self-esteem,' and it is the assertion that when we really learn to trust – and trust is called 'possibility thinking' – then, whereas we used to think of ourselves as failures, we now find our egos uplifted and we see endless possibilities in ourselves. 'Jesus never called any person a sinner, the cross of Christ sanctifies your ego-trip.'

Do I need to say that this is the exact opposite of Bible truth? What the Bible tells us is that there is no possibility of getting anywhere with God until we face up to what we are, and what we are is very bad indeed.

Jacob, in his days of disobedience and self-confidence, would have gone a long way on the 'gospel of success' television shows, but when he met himself by the brook Jabbok he began to get somewhere with God.

Look at the story. It begins with Jacob alone and frightened, facing the mess created by his own selfishness and dishonesty.

It reaches the central climax when he clings to a dark figure in the night and cries – verse 26 – 'I will not let you go unless you bless me.' And it ends with the poignant picture of verse 31: the sun rising over a limping man, his physical strength broken and his faith renewed, and his name changed from Jacob – supplanter, cheat, wide-boy, con-man (that is what 'Jacob' means) to Israel – a prince with God, a powerful prevailer with God, someone to whom God hearkens as a king to his princely son.

Let me give you a few phrases in the form of slogans, to sum up the story. Here is the first.

Man's worst enemy is himself, and a woman's worst enemy is herself

Jacob really is a puzzle of course. What was the secret of this man? He had a spiritual vision, but much of the time he was a carnal man. That is the strange tension in Jacob. He saw good ends – and that makes it clear that he was indeed a child of God – but he sought them by bad means – that showed how carnal he was.

In chapter 32, leading up to our story, his vision taught him that 'The angel of God encampeth round them that fear him', and that gave him the idea of that magnificent pun calling that place *Ma-ha-naim* – two camps, the camp I live in and the camp around me of the protection of God. But chapter 33 shows his carnality taking over again, plunging him into elaborate schemes to avoid his brother's vengeance.

That is Jacob, you see. He has just learnt that the angel

of God encamps around him, but 'I'm going to be a belt-and-braces man – two belts and three pairs of braces – I'm going to depend on a lot of other things as well.'

But that night, Jacob got his come-uppance. He has planned all he can, but now he is left alone sitting on a boulder, scrambling disconsolately by the stream, the water roaring its sound in his ears like the accusing roar of his conscience.

Whether in the body or out of the body, Jacob could afterwards never tell, but such a night of terror and battle he never before spent. It was Esau, and it was not Esau; it was God and it was not God; it was both God and Esau.

Jacob never knew who the terrible wrestler really was, until, just before morning broke, with one last wrench, he was left lame for life. Then, as if from the open heaven, he was baptised by the gracious wrestler into a new name – for the mysterious man said to Jacob as he lay helpless, 'Your name shall no longer be called Jacob, but Israel, for you have striven with God and with man.'

Jacob at last faced up to the enemy that he had been running away from. He faced up to the fact that his enemy was himself.

What do you have to face when you look at yourself? A past sin which you cannot forgive even though God has forgiven it? A present besetting sin which clings to you so easily? A shrinking nature which makes you dismiss any idea of usefulness to God? A vulnerable or demanding situation in which you cannot bring yourself to trust God? Have you discovered yourself, as your own worst enemy?

Bad times can be God's best

Like Jacob, as long as things go well, we can settle in half-hearted commitment, or even carnality, satisfied with self. In fact that can keep us from God altogether.

It may well be there are people here who have never yet been born again, people who have never yet fled to Christ because you are satisfied with yourself.

And so often those of us who have made that discovery at any rate, and have fled from ourselves in the hope of salvation to the sinner's Saviour – so often we have then become satisfied again.

How long ago did we older Christians dismiss the possibility that there might still be something to learn, and still some character improvement possible in the purposes of God?

So God stops things going well for us, and He takes things away from us, and, verse 24, 'Jacob was left alone.' – 'My company has gone on before and I am left alone with thee.'

Ponder on that and see if that fits your situation. Has God taken something off you lately? In actual fact, it may be the best thing that can happen to you – bad times can be the highway to God's best.

Thirdly, another little slogan.

Come to yourself and you are not far from God

Remember the prodigal son? Intriguingly, the 'far country' that he went to was precisely the place where the brook Jabbok is – Dacapolis, the ten cities, the bright lights on the other side of Galilee – the far country.

That is where Jacob was physically and is spiritually now.

Father's son, or Satan's swineherd? 'What on earth am I doing here?' he asks himself. And Jesus says 'When he came to himself . . .' then it was a tremendous step towards coming to God.

The frightening figure said to Jacob as he wrestled with him (verse 27) 'What is your name?' Name means identity:

'What does your name represent? What is your identity?'

And when we are compelled to look at ourselves, the wrestling match begins, because God is getting close to us. Are you a new Christian? Have you just begun to follow Christ and trust Him? You may say 'It is very odd, I am struggling now more than I was before.' (*Cf.* Romans 7:21.) That's right! Well done, that's splendid! It is a sign that you are really born again. It is when we begin to see ourselves as we are that we begin to get somewhere with God, and we should not be surprised at inner conflict.

Now there is something to fight about. We older Christians, let us be very merciful, and very patient with these new converts; they are going to bring the most hair-raising problems that you did not even know existed, and it is no good saying 'You shouldn't be in them!' because they are in them, and God has saved them in them. They so much need your love and your pastoring and your nurture and your understanding. 'Come to yourself, and you are not far from God.'

Cast down, but cast on Him

When I read verse 25 I have a fellow-feeling for Jacob, because I suffer from a thing called a sacro-iliac lesion. I have had it for about twenty-five years. I do not know what any one of those words means, but I know it is very painful, and it has got to do a great deal with the back, the left hip, and the left leg. Sometimes I am simply crying with pain, and the depression it brings – not very often, but sometimes, it can be as bad as that. Much more often – and I say this from my heart – I thank God for it.

How often you see, God has caught me, when, through pride, I am on the verge of becoming unuseable and insufferable; and God, for reasons that I cannot understand, has so often blessed my ministry that I start getting so proud and insufferable, then down I go on my back.

And lying on my back for a fortnight, God says, 'Who matters?' and I have to say, 'That I should walk humbly with You Lord, thank You, thank You.'

And then He says, 'Tell me your name.' And I say, 'Don Bridge; silly, scheming, sinful, selfish Don Bridge.'

And then He says, and it is such bliss, 'Don Bridge, My grace is sufficient for you. My strength is made perfect in weakness.'

And I really mean it, I am not just saying it for effect, I really do thank Him. It is a lovely thorn in the flesh, I am so grateful.

When He has shown us our name, we can begin to ask Him His name.

'Tell me your name,' says Jacob, 'now that I have admitted my own.' Jacob knows it in his heart, so he says, in verse 30, 'I have seen God.' He knew all along, or at least he suspected who was wrestling with him.

And, you know, when we take a good look at ourselves and what we are, for the first time we are in some condition to look at God and what He is, because – what is He? – He is the sinner's Saviour, and there is nothing to look at in Him and nothing to listen to in Him until you learn to call yourself a sinner again; supremely, the sinner's Saviour.

Wesley carries this triumphantly onto the New Testament revelation, that God's name is love – what is your name? – love to the loveless.

> Yield to me now for I am weak,
> But confident in self-despair . . .

He imagines Jacob and you and me crying.

Speak to my heart, in blessings speak:
Be conquered by my instant prayer:
Speak, or Thou never hence shall move,
And tell me if Thy name is love.

And the certainty will come to you:

'Tis love, 'tis love! Thou diest for me,
I hear Thy whisper in my heart!
The morning breaks, the shadows flee,
Pure, universal love Thou art . . .
Jesus, the feeble sinner's friend:
Nor wilt Thou with the night depart,
But stay and love me to the end;
Thy mercies never shall remove;
Thy nature and Thy name is love.

What a discovery! Shown my weakness and my wretched-
ness, and my mixed motives, and my uncleanness – in order
to be shown the immeasurable love of God.

Let me finish with two pictures.

The first – verse 31 – when it was all over, 'The sun rose
on Jacob as he passed . . .'

And the second is Wesley's final words on the story.

The Sun of Righteousness on me
Hath risen, with healing in His wings;
Withered my nature's strength, from Thee
My soul its life and succour brings;
My help is all laid up above;
Thy nature and Thy name is love.
Contented now, upon my thigh
I halt till life's short journey end;

All helplessness, all weakness, I
On Thee alone for strength depend . . .
Through all eternity to prove
Thy nature and Thy name is love.

In the words of F.B. Meyer, who finishes an account of this story with this question:

Have you abandoned the art of self-defence
For the artlessness of clinging trust?

'MY GRACE IS SUFFICIENT'

by Rev Kenneth Prior

2 Corinthians 12:7–10

From our reading, I'd just like to read one of the verses again – verse 9. This verse describes those great resources which are within the reach of every single Christian believer. It begins with the source of sufficiency, God's grace. And then the perfection of power, 'in our weakness'; and then as a consequence of that, the boasting of the believer.

The source of sufficiency

Paul says that this is something which God said to him: 'He said to me.' In fact he uses the perfect tense – 'He has said to me.' Paul is aware that this is something not that God is just saying to him now, but something which God has said to him in the past – a great truth which as a Christian he already knew before he went through the experience described in these verses, and which ought to be the common assumption of every Christian believer; and that is the basic presuppositon about the grace of God.

Whatever may be the perplexity through which we pass, whatever the questionings there may be in our minds, there's one basic fixed point and that is God's grace towards us, and that of course is something which Paul emphasised in different ways again and again. Everything which was good about him, he attributed not to himself but to the favour with which God looked at him, a favour which Paul did not, for one moment, deserve.

Hear for example how he describes his conversion. What does he say? 'Suddenly I exercised my great intelligence'? No, he doesn't say that at all. 'When God, who set me apart from birth and called me by his grace, was pleased to reveal his Son in me . . .' (*cf.* Gal. 1:15–16). It wasn't a sudden change of heart or a sudden stroke of genius on his part to which he attributed what happened to him, but the fact God looked upon him with a favour which was the last thing that he deserved, and simply revealed the Lord Jesus Christ, not just *to* him, but actually *in* him. God, in the sovereignty of His grace, broke into his life and did something for Paul which he could never discover by his own insight or intelligence.

He spoke in exactly the same way about his subsequent service. 'By the grace of God I am what I am . . .' (1 Cor. 15:10). Though he could rightly point to tremendous exertions ('I worked harder than any of them'), yet it was with the rider, 'Not I, but the grace of God which is with me.' He owed everything to God's favour towards him.

I wonder if that is how you view yourself. All that is good about you in the eyes of God, you owe to the fact that God, in a way that you could never deserve, decided to smile upon you and look upon you with favour. This was a truth which Paul already knew, which now came especially into its own, because of the circumstances in which he found himself.

He was undergoing something of a crisis. He had the great problem of offering a prayer to which he did not seem to get the answer that he wanted. He had been wrestling in prayer with God over his weaknesses. And what was God's word to him? It was a reminder that God had already said to him, 'My grace is sufficient for you,' and that was what mattered more than anything.

There were many things which he could not understand about this 'thorn in the flesh', but there was one thing that mattered more to him than anything else, and that was that God was smiling upon him. Isn't that wonderful? If we were to look around this tent tonight and ask people to stand up and say what was bothering them, I think we would find a whole host of problems in people's lives. If I detected what God was doing last night, some of us were facing up to facts about ourselves as we were reminded about what happened to Jacob. We began to look at ourselves perhaps, as God sees us, and that is very disturbing indeed.

We have the perfect Advocate. The perfect response to anything that God may have said to us last night is in the Lord Jesus Christ. That is why we can afford to face up to ourselves. May I just remind you that in spite of all that, God is smiling upon you tonight? He looks upon you, not in the way that you deserve, but according to His grace. And Paul says here the great thing that's so precious to him is this, that it is sufficient, the fact that God looks upon you with favour. You and I may sometimes find ourselves defeated by our sins, but God is never defeated. As Paul says in Romans, 'Where sin increased, grace [notice that word again] abounded all the more.' The greater our need, the more God can exercise His grace towards us.

It may be that some of us didn't need to come to Keswick to have a feeling of failure and guilt. I'm quite sure in a crowd of people like this, I'm talking to some parents whose great problem is that they are deeply worried about their children. It isn't easy bringing up children, particularly in the teenage years, is it? Some of you have got children who have gone beyond that age. They are a bitter disappointment and you see other people rejoicing, telling you what their children are doing in the Lord's service. And it causes such a sinking feeling inside you, because you say, 'If only my children . . .', and then you begin to look back and you say, 'Where did I go wrong?' It's so easy to feel guilty.

May I just remind you of something? God smiles on you. And that is sufficient for you, even though you don't seem to be getting the kind of answer to your prayer that you would really like, yet you do know this, because you have the assurance of God's Word – He smiles upon you in favour; and faith, because you respond to God's grace by faith, is sufficient for you. Will you accept that? Say in your heart: 'Yes Lord, even though I long to get the answer I want to my prayers, yet I realise that you look upon me in favour, not because I deserve it. I may have made mistakes, yes Lord; but You still look upon me in favour, and how I glory and rejoice in that!'

Many years ago, a man I used to know who was active in God's work failed rather badly and disappeared from the Christian scene. He had to, it would have been difficult for him to continue in the work he was doing. I suppose I must have forgotten all about him. And then one day I was at a Convention and I met him – he was the last person I expected to see at that Christian Convention. I was surprised, probably as much as anyone, to see him there. What he could have said was 'I've repented,' and that would have been quite true. But he said to me, 'You are looking at a man on whom the Lord has had mercy.'

As far as this moment is concerned, what matters most of all is that God looks upon you in grace and favour, and that should be sufficient for you.

Would you also notice another significance of that tense, the perfect tense. It is not only something which is settled in the past, but a perfect tense always has a sort of present significance – 'He has said to me.' It is still true now and it goes on being true, and how suitable that is for any declaration about the grace of God! It means that God's grace is still sufficient, and it goes on being sufficient.

God's grace never fails, there is something abiding about it. Our relationship with God is based on what has sometimes been called 'The covenant of God's grace', a covenant that He will never break, a grace that never fails. In our extremity, we might well be just like the psalmist. How wonderful the psalms are! They are written by real men who actually say the kind of things that sometimes we would not dare to say. And the psalmist once cried out 'Has God forgotten to be gracious?'

We know the answer. God would never forget to be gracious.

It is expressed in a lovely way by Augustus Toplady, the 'saintly sinner', an eighteenth-century evangelical leader with many problems.

> My name from the palms of His hand
> Eternity will not erase
> Impressed on His heart it remains,
> In marks of indelible grace.

'I have said.' Nothing can change it, because God's grace is indelible, and that's the grace of God which is sufficient for you. Yes, that is the first great truth that we find set before us here. The source of our sufficiency is God's grace.

The perfection of God's power

The Greek word for 'thorn' originally denoted something

pointed. That is the use that predominates in the Greek translation of the Old Testament. It may well have been a physical ailment. The New English Bible, with characteristic freedom, renders it 'a sharp physical pain'. There are many suggestions as to what it was – eye trouble, recurring malaria, epilepsy; and it has been used to demonstrate that God does not always grant physical healing in answer to our prayers when we are unwell.

That would, of course, have a very meaningful application to God's promise. And we had a wonderful example last night, didn't we, of the fact that when Jacob's thigh was put out of joint in the days before plastic joints and all the rest of it, it meant that for the rest of his days, he had that as a 'thorn in the flesh' in his body, which would have the ministry to him that Paul's thorn would have here.

Some think it was something spiritual, or at least that it was something more than just bodily. It doesn't say 'in', which is a natural word to use if referring to his physical body. It is a thorn 'for the flesh', and of course the word 'flesh' in Paul's writings nearly always refers to something much more than just our physical body. It refers to our human nature in its weakness through being fallen. Paul didn't write literally 'a thorn in my body', and there is a perfectly good Greek word for the word 'body', which he could have used.

It is also 'a messenger of Satan' – a device of his to exploit our fleshly weakness. The Reformers and the early Fathers felt that the thorn was spiritual in character. But whatever we say, even if it was actually a physical affliction, there is some real spiritual significance in it, and it has a moral connotation as well. It was an occasion to sin, it was something which the devil could use. Satan was playing on Paul's human weaknesses.

Romans 7 shows us how sin can take up residence in the

flesh where it can exploit all our fleshly weaknesses. That is why so many sins can be accounted for and described psychologically. If you lose your temper, it is because you are inadequate, insecure, or just tired. That is the fleshly weakness; sin, when taking up residence in your members, can exploit difficult circumstances, can lay you open to temptation.

Paul had something in his life, and whatever it was, illness, difficult circumstances, a personal weakness, he said that 'If only it could be removed from me, I could be a much better Christian.' And so three times he asked God to remove it. And the answer he got was that 'My grace is sufficient for you.' That he is reminded of again and again. This is the way we prove the sufficiency of God's grace.

'The way made perfect' means literally, 'To achieve its purpose'. The way God's power achieves its purpose in us is so often through our weaknesses. Not by being angels who have never known a fallen world like this, but in the situation of human weakness.

I'm not suggesting that we should say 'Lord, lead us into temptation.' We naturally shrink from it. It is very often when we are aware of our weakness that we prove God's power the most. The grass always looks so much greener on the other side of the fence, doesn't it? But God says 'No, stay where you are, because that is where you are going to prove my power, and it is going to work out and achieve its purpose, there where you now are.'

So we see the second great truth. The second great milestone, as we go through this verse, is the perfection of God's power that 'My power is made perfect in weakness.' What then is going to be our consequent attitude?

The boasting of the believer

Don't misread Paul here. He does not say 'I'm going to

boast about my failings.' It is not a case of 'continuing in sin that grace may abound,' but rather 'I'm going to boast in my weaknesses.' And it doesn't mean that Paul is going to seek suffering as the ascetics did – sleeping on beds of nails and wearing hair shirts and things of that sort.

But he says, 'A thorn was given me in the flesh.' It wasn't something he sought. We are not to plan this deliberately – 'Let's make life really difficult for myself so that I can prove God's power.' No. It was something which was given to him, something which the devil did, which God in His over-riding sovereignty, was able to repeatedly turn what the devil was doing to His sovereign purpose.

'A thorn was given me in the flesh.' The purpose is, that the power of Christ may rest upon me, literally, 'pitch His tent upon me'; may dwell in me like a tent, just as the *shekinah* glory of old dwelt in the Old Testament tabernacle. This happens when we admit our weaknesses. Phillip Hughes says in his great commentary on 2 Corinthians, 'The greater the servant's weakness, the more conspicuous is the power of the Master's all sufficient grace.'

Early in this chapter, Paul made reference to a great spiritual experience that God had given him. But we see what God had to do with him (verse 7). 'To keep me from being too elated' – or, as the NIV puts it much more bluntly, 'To keep me from becoming conceited' – 'a thorn was given me in the flesh.' So the apostle says 'I will all the more gladly boast, not of this tremendous spiritual experience that I've had which makes me a cut above the other Christians [some people love doing that, don't they!]. No; that is not what I glory in, but in the weaknesses that God in His sovereignty has allowed me to have.' That was what Paul had to learn.

One of the tragedies of today is the way in which the devil can so often ruin what may well be genuine blessings of the

Spirit of God. And they become the cause of elitism which provokes the most unhappy divisions in our churches. But God has to remind us of our weakness if His power is to rest upon us.

It was actually from this very platform that a speaker once said of the expression 'the fullness of the Holy Spirit', that it is commended and exemplified in Scripture but never claimed. You never find any of these men of God saying, 'Well, I'm filled with the Spirit.' Being human, he might well have said, 'Well I've had this great experience that makes me rather a special Christian.' He was prevented from that. He says, 'What I boast in and glory in is the fact that I'm an ordinary, weak human being. Yet it is due to the fact that I'm an ordinary, weak human being that I prove the power of God.' One of the besetting sins of evangelicals is spiritual pride.

Pride has caused revival to go wrong. Some of you I hope have read *Dynamics of Spiritual Life*, by Richard Lovelace. He has a chapter in which he discusses the writings of Jonathan Edwards, about the New England revival, showing how revivals can go wrong. The trouble is, the flesh can get in and involve us in this 'holier than thou' attitude which can be so deeply offensive to others.

It can, for example, close Christians' minds to the Word of God. They think they know it all. Are you like that? Are the people in your church like that?

We can indeed be in the same danger that Paul was in of being too elated by the abundance of revelations, too elated by the fact that we are evangelicals, and so on, forgetting the fact that it is only the mercy of God that has brought us into contact with these great truths. Sometimes God has to deal with successful Christian workers in this way. Sometimes this is the way that God's power is made perfect. And so Paul says 'I boast of my weaknesses because this is where I prove God's power.' God uses the sins of others to do this for us. Is someone here tonight who is smarting with resentment against someone? Is there some minister who is smarting with resentment against those who criticise him?

Is that what God is doing for any of us here tonight, wanting to prove that His grace to you is sufficient, to prove His power to you? And in order to do that He had to bring you face to face with your own weaknesses. Then instead of saying 'Oh dear, I wish I wasn't like that,' could we learn to glorify God for it? These very weaknesses I gladly accept, because it is in this very context that I can prove again and again that God's favour towards me is what matters most of all. And this is the very area in which, by that grace, I can prove the power of God.

Yes, Paul had very different ideas when he offered that prayer to God. 'God has said to me "My grace is sufficient for you, my power is made perfect in weakness."' So Paul responds to God's Word – 'I will all the more gladly boast of my weaknesses that the power of Christ may rest upon me.'

'BUT ONE LORD'
by Mr Alan Nute

1 Corinthians 8:6

The first commentary that I acquired as a young Christian was the seventh of eight volumes of the *Commentary on Holy Scripture* edited by C.J. Ellicott. The particular volume covered Acts to Galatians.

I decided, when I came into possession of that book, that I would work through 1 Corinthians with it at my elbow. At the conclusion of the commentator's introduction to the epistle, I came across a paragraph which made an unforgettable impression upon me. I'd like to read it to you.

> Many of the subjects treated of here were local and personal; the combination of circumstances which gave rise to them cannot possibly occur again in Christendom, but the principles on which the apostle decided these matters are imperishable and of universal obligation. They can guide the church amid the complex civilisation of the present century as truly and as clearly as they indicated to her the path of safety in the infancy of the Christian faith.

The language may be dated. But I am more than ever convinced of the accuracy and the helpfulness of that particular paragraph, especially as it relates to the verses that we have before us. The circumstances are completely different; in particular in relation to this matter of food sacrificed to idols – well, that's a world away from our own. But the principles upon which the apostle supplies guidance for the Corinthian believers – those principles are as relevant as ever.

Now Corinth, as we have been reminded in our morning Bible readings, was a centre of trade and commerce. Like a magnet, it drew people from every corner of the world. The population of Corinth was truly cosmopolitan. Cults of every conceivable kind flourished there, and in addition the city gained for itself the most unenviable reputation for being a centre of vice and evil of the worst possible kind.

In many respects Corinth can be said to correspond more closely to the situation in Britain today than almost any of the other New Testament cities. As a result new Christians in Corinth found themselves confronted by a very real dilemma. How should they relate to their former associates? Their pre-conversion, non-Christian friends and relatives? Those still worshipped the old gods. They still followed what the believers now regarded as thoroughly objectionable pagan practices. Should they shun them, or should they not?

Some felt that this was the safest and wisest course to take – to sever all links with such people. How else, they argued, could one keep oneself unspotted from the world? Others, however, saw things differently. They said, 'To segregate ourselves from our non-Christian friends is wholly unnecessary. Indeed, it would be quite wrong.'

The risks, they contended, were more imaginary than real. And in any case, they added, what about the believer's obligation to be light and salt in the world?

Now it seems to me to be fairly clear that it was this latter group that raised the whole matter with the apostle. Their position is summed up in what was probably two quotes from their letter to Paul, found in verse 4: 'An idol is nothing at all in the world' (or as the NIV puts it, 'has no real existence'). And again: 'There is no God but one.'

Well, at least we can say this; that the apostle Paul would have agreed with them that an idol is nothing in the world. In other words, it is nothing that the worshipper thinks it to be. In other words – the whole thing is sham.

I am quite sure that he, together with them, would have agreed with Isaiah's satire on idols and idolatry. Remember how he mocked the whole idea? He said, the people come and they chop down a tree. Half of the wood of that tree they burn on the fire. Over it – and I quote – 'He prepares his meal, he roasts his meat and eats his fill. He also warms himself and says, "Ah! I am warm; I see the fire." From the rest he makes a god, his idol; he bows down to it and worships it. He prays to it and says, "Save me; you are my god."' (Isaiah 44:16–17).

No! An idol has no power whatsoever either to confer good or to inflict evil. It needs neither to be respected nor feared. Says the apostle, 'These are so-called gods. Gods in name but not in nature. There is no God but one.'

Yet in our world as in Corinth there are many gods and many lords. Many were the gods that were worshipped; many are the gods that are worshipped today. And the idols are not necessarily of wood or stone or metal, but far more subtle are the idols that are erected in the human heart and before which the worshipper bows. There are many gods and there are many lords who are served.

And so it almost seems as if the apostle in the same

breath both denies and acknowledges their existence. Perhaps they are a little bit like masks, worn by the bank robber. Of itself the idol, like the mask, is nothing; and yet lurking behind it sinister and evil forces operate. Now; what is the solution, for the Christian living in such a situation? Should the policy be one of withdrawal and separation? 'Wholly unnecessary,' says one group. 'Absolutely vital,' says the other.

How does the apostle answer it? Well, you must read the succeeding chapters and see, for his answer is very extensive. But it is significant that he doesn't come down firmly on either side. From his answer, however, I want to extract just one statement. I believe it to be a statement of such significance that if it were believed and acted upon it would be enough to resolve the whole problem. Indeed, I think I could go further and say that if it were to be acted upon it could solve every problem for the child of God. And this is the statement which is my text for you tonight. 'For us . . . there is but one Lord, Jesus Christ, through whom all things came and through whom we live' (8:6).

Let but the Christian hold that tenaciously, let him but respond to that appropriately and all will be well. In the sentence the two words 'for us' are emphatic, and we need to make them emphatic too. Whatever gods men may worship, whatever lords they may serve, for us there is but one Lord, unique and incomparable.

He is unique in three ways.

He is unique in the person that He is

'For us there is but one Lord, Jesus Christ' – possessed of true humanity and full deity. Who is this one Lord? His name is Jesus. The Jesus who was born at Bethlehem, who lived at Nazareth and laboured there. The Jesus who sat wearily at a well-side and craved from a Samaritan woman a drink of water, for he was hot and tired and thirsty. The Jesus who healed the sick, gave sight to the blind, cleansed the leper, raised the dead. The Jesus who in Gethsemane sweated as it were great drops of blood falling down to the ground. The Jesus who, thorn-crowned, nailed to a cross, died in agony and shame.

For us there is but one Lord, Jesus. The Jesus who was raised again on the third day. The Jesus who gave many convincing proofs that He was alive. Of whom Peter was able to say, 'We ate and drank with Him after He rose from the dead.' The Jesus who is exalted and sits at the right hand of the Father on high. For us there is but one Lord, and His name is Jesus. And He is the Christ. The One from of old; the anointed One. Not only sent by God, but come from God. This is the Christ in whom all the divinely inspired Old Testament expectations have their meanings.

Some of you remember the days of war, when a siren would sound and you would wait and presently there would come that distinctive, uncanny throb of the German warplane. Then a searchlight would spring into action and begin to search the night sky. And others would join it and they would criss-cross the sky until one would isolate the plane, and then all would come together and converge upon it.

So it is with all the Old Testament prophets and the Psalmist. They sweep the night sky of Scripture. And at length He comes, and they all focus on Him – Jesus, the Christ. So all these strands of messianic prophecy find their focus in Him, the Lord Jesus Christ, the promised prophet and priest and king; Son of Man, Son of God.

Increasingly in the New Testament the term Christ is associated with His deity. Peter confesses, 'You are the Christ, the Son of the living God.' Martha similarly: 'I

believe that you are the Christ, the Son of God who is to
come into the world.' And so we gladly confess Him and say
– and I trust my words find an echo in your hearts, even
though you do not speak them with me – the words of the
apostle, 'for us'.

It doesn't matter about the rest. They have their many
gods and their many lords. We think of them. We pray for
them. We go forth to preach to them. But for us there is but
one Lord, Jesus Christ, unique in the person He is.

He is unique in the authority He wields

Earlier in the same verse the apostle declared, 'For us there
is but one God, the Father, from whom all things came.'
God the Father is the source of all creation. But then he
adds, 'And there is but one Lord Jesus Christ, through
whom all things came . . .' He, the Lord Jesus Christ, is the
agent in all creation. So Paul echoes the familar words of
John when he wrote 'Through him all things were made,
and without him nothing was made that was made.' Similarly, the writer to the Hebrews: 'Through whom, that is
His Son, He made the universe'. And so ultimately everything and everyone owed their existence to Him. It is by His
power that all came into being. It is through – whose
power? His power – all is upheld.

There are many examples. See Him stand in the prow of
a little storm-tossed vessel on Galilee, the rain lashing
down and the wind blowing and far worse. Then He says,
'Peace, be still.' The wild waves are hushed and the angry
deep sinks like a child to sleep. 'Through whom all things
came' – disease and death retreat at His word; demons
quake before Him and instantly yield to His authority.
Risen from the dead He declares, 'All authority in heaven
and on earth has been vested in Me.' And He demonstrates

the fact, for barred doors and windows prove no obstacle to Him.

Distances obliterated, time and space, which circumscribe our lives and hold us within their confines, lose all significance for Him, for all authority in heaven and on earth is given to Him. All things, material and physical, natural and supernatural, human, angelic and demonic, all are under His control. He is King of kings and Lord of lords. King of all kings, for it is only through Him that they come to power, and only through Him do they remain in power. Lord of all lords, for by Him alone do they exercise their subordinate authority. He stands supreme, alone, unique in the person that He is, unique in the authority that He wields.

But thirdly . . .

He is unique in the life that He communicates

'Through whom we live' – not only is He the One through whom all creation came into being, He is the One through whom redemption has been brought to men. By His word a universe is begotten; by His death His church is born. It is to Him and to Him alone that we owe this new and eternal life that we possess. But more, it is in association with Him that we live.

'Through whom we live' – as branches in one vine; as members in one body; His life flows in us; His life sustains us and His life guarantees our eternal life, one with Himself. I cannot die, my soul is purchased with His blood, my life is hid with Christ on high, with Christ, my Saviour and my God.

And so, my dear brothers and sisters,. against the background of a pluralistic society, when men and women tragically bow down and worship many gods, when men and women sadly serve many lords and owe their allegiance to them, this is your confession – I am convinced – as it is mine. 'For us, for us there is but one Lord, Jesus Christ, through whom all things came and through whom we live.'

Is that going to be but a credal statement? Is that all it's going to be? Should we not rather allow it to be that truth, that reality that sets us free from needless fear of those alien powers, real or imaginary? Is the fear of the many gods and the many lords going to cripple and restrict? Shall we not recognise that for us, there is but one?

To that one Lord, unique in His person and in His authority as also in the life that He communicates, let us resolve to bring a submission; a commitment; an obedience that is complete, unquestioning and lifelong – until that glad day when we see Him. And then our submission and our commitment and our obedience to Him, the one Lord, will be eternal.

IS JESUS LORD?

by Rev Philip Hacking

Matthew 7:21–23

'Jesus is Lord' is an affirmation that I hope we believe; the very first credal statement. It's already been brought to us by Alan this evening. But I want to begin by changing the words round a little: 'Is Jesus Lord?'

There's nothing we can do or not do tonight that can ever change the fact that He is Lord. You don't make Him Lord; He *is* Lord whatever you do. Whether you neglect or not, He is the Son of God – He's been declared to be that by the resurrection from the dead. He's at the right hand of power, and one day He comes and every knee will bow and every tongue confess He's Lord. So He is; but the point of a convention is that all that's real and true should be real for us.

Let us read from Matthew chapter 7, towards the end of the Sermon on the Mount. The penultimate paragraph of a great sermon. 'He who does the will of my Father who is in heaven' (Matt. 7:21). That, for Jesus, is the equivalent of really saying and meaning Jesus is Lord. Has it seemed strange to you that whenever you say the Lord's Prayer, you make the petition, 'Your will be done'? Why? Won't His will be done? Isn't He the sovereign God? Yet it's true, we have a part to play in the doing of the will of God.

For example, we are told to pray for it. It's a mystery, isn't it. I still don't understand how it works. But in some way, God takes those prayers and makes them part of His purpose, and that's why earlier in the Sermon on the Mountain (Matt. 6:8), Jesus says, 'Your Father knows what you need before you ask him.' – Pray then! He doesn't say, 'Well God knows exactly what's going to happen to you, so no need to bother praying.'

You pray. And when you pray, your prayer becomes like that boomerang that comes back to you and hits you. Do you remember the Old Testament prayer of Nehemiah, who discovered that things had gone wrong with the world? He prayed to God, 'God, do something about Jerusalem.' He prayed with a tremendous fervency that somewhere, somehow, God would find somebody to turn the tide. And by the time he got to the end of that prayer, he was saying, 'Lord, give me grace.' The prayer had hit back to him.

You can't pray about a world that is without Christ and a world that's languishing in need, without some response from the individual's heart. When we think of the lordship of Jesus, and when we begin to pray for a world of need, that His will may be done, it comes home to us.

Can I point out to you, from Scripture, that it's possible to frustrate God's will? I don't care how stern a Calvinist you are, it's possible to frustrate God's will. Jesus said so and He was never wrong. In Luke 7:30, He said of some people that they frustrated God's purpose. The Pharisees refused the message of John the Baptist. They would not repent, and what God had meant for them they never knew, because they frustrated God's purpose.

Or I go back to the Old Testament character, Lot, who, it says, 'Vexed his righteous soul from day to day in evil Sodom' (2 Pet. 2:8); he was dragged out and saved – just –

by fire. Did God mean Lot to be vexing His righteous soul? Never! He was frustrating God's will for his life and he was saved – just! My fear is, there are some people in this tent who will be saved – just! You'll be there by the skin of your teeth. But when the books are out, what you've done on earth won't take a great deal of totting up. I don't want to be there – just!

I believe it's the will of God that you and I should obey the lordship of Jesus. And do it joyfully. One of the great things about our Lord, is that He did God's will joyfully. 'I seek not my own will, but the will of him who sent me,' He says. When He had been talking to the woman at the well and the disciples couldn't understand why He was elated, He said 'My meat, my food, is to do the will of him that sent me, and to finish the work.' It was meat and drink to Him. I wonder if I do speak to some, I guess I do, who sort of do God's will, who painfully and with grim obligation do it. I see a Saviour who delighted to do it. In the Garden of Gethsemane Jesus still could say, 'Not my will but yours be done.'

Let me therefore take, out of these words of Jesus, something of what it means to do God's will. I'm sure you know the Sermon on the Mount very well, and I'm sure you know it ends with lots of clear contrasts. Two roads, two fruits, two destinations, two foundations. No middle ground and these tremendously stark words that He says to us.

On the highway signs, in the good old days when they had words, there were two words that I think stand across this paragraph – NO ENTRY – ONE WAY. Simple as that. As I read this word 'No Entry', I see Jesus giving three negatives. 'Not everyone . . .' – and from the negative, I get the message about the lordship of Jesus. First of all . . .

It's more than believing

'Not everyone who says "Lord"' – that's right theology. We as a Convention are built on that theology, and we are not ashamed of it. He is the Son of God. He is risen from the dead. He will come again. He is Lord – but it's more than that.

Saul of Tarsus, even before he became a Christian, knew it on the Damascus road. He asked two questions, you remember them? 'Who are you, Lord?' 'I'm Jesus.' 'Lord, what do you want me to do?' And I submit to you that you may not ask the first question without the second. If in your heart of hearts you have acknowledged that Jesus is Lord and you've got your belief in the right place and you're unashamed – dare you ask the question 'Lord, what do you want me to do?' Is it possible that we're not prepared to go through with the implication of what that means?

It may be something dramatic. It may be that clear sense of the call of God, and you've so far been running away from it. Or maybe it was just in general terms about the thrust of your life. But are you really submitting to the authority of Jesus? You may not call Him Lord, and disobey Him. Or bring it to another level. Here is Jesus, washing the disciple's feet, and He says, in John 13:13, 'You call me "Master" and "Lord", and you do well, for so I am. If I'm your Lord and Master and I've washed your feet, you also ought to wash one another's feet.'

He is calling you to go into the world and show the difference. There's going to be no fruit from any evangelism unless Christians live as if He were Lord. 'More than believing.'

Do you remember dear Peter? Dear Peter! He was an honest sort of guy was Peter. Jesus gave a vision to him in Acts chapter 10, and He said to Peter 'Rise, Peter, kill and eat, go on, the Gentile world is waiting for you, forget your taboos.' And Peter said – you remember those famous words – 'No, Lord'. I submit to you, you can never say those words. They cancel each other out. You either say 'Yes, Lord,' or you say 'No.' But you don't say 'No, Lord.' You get my meaning? How many of us are saying 'No, Lord: I'm prepared to go so far – but not that; don't disturb me there, Lord'?

It's more than praising

It's important that the words come together. 'Not everyone who says to me Lord, Lord,' – the fervency. And to get it across, He says it twice again, in verse 22 – 'On that day, many will say Lord, Lord.' A note of fervency.

I hope you understand what I mean when I say you can have a convention that stands for right belief – and the congregation can be sound asleep as well. I for the life of me cannot understand why you can't have right theology and fervent praising together. It's always seemed right to me; it's the deep things of God that make me want to well out in praise. Listening to the Bible readings this week, they're doing me a world of good. How we ministers need to be ministered to! As I hear the Bible readings, and I'm being enthused by those great chapters, out of me comes a well, I want to sing praise, because of the sheer depth of the Word of God. Let's never be the kind of convention that's sound and solid and dead.

Don't you want to say 'Lord, Lord'? Don't you enjoy praising God? I hope you feel that's right in a convention. I think it is. The note of thanksgiving. God inhabits the praises of His people. Oh! I know the other danger and that's what Jesus is saying. There's a danger of empty mindless praise.

By all means, praise Jesus as Lord; by all means say 'Lord, Lord' – providing you mean what you sing. I wonder if God keeps a record of all the things we've sung to Him. How many thousands tell Him how much they love Him. I guess He looks down with unbelief on some of us, for 'If you love Me, you'll keep My commandments.'

How often have you sung your allegiance? How often have you sung your dedication? Where's it ended? There are still people, I really think, who imagine that God looks down on a Keswick Convention, on a Sunday morning service, and what He sees is just that moment. Then He switches off and He doesn't bother what you do for the rest of the year. And they imagine that we show how much we love Him by the fervency with which we sing.

But the level of my fervency doesn't prove the reality and integrity of my living. Don't you get the point? God is not going to say 'Ah yes, John over there is a marvellous Christian, did you see how he was singing that hymn?' He'll say 'John over there is a marvellous Christian, look how he lives! Look how he obeys!' More than believing. More than praising.

It's more than doing

There are people who are quite happy thus far. The practical Christians who say 'Yes, I've not got too much time for all this doctrine, I really don't go very much on all this worship, I'm one of these down to earth people, helping your neighbour, doing to them as you'd want them to do to you.' Oh, listen to Jesus. 'Many in that day will say, "Did we not prophesy? Did we not cast out demons? Did we not do, do, do?"' And I find it staggering that our Lord will say to them 'Depart from me, you evildoers.' Now there's no doubt these people did do these things. Therefore they're not liars, but you see, they were depending on their doing.

May I say again – doing is vital. The Keswick Convention

should always be linked with practical holiness. It's not just to do with what happens in these tents, it's what happens when we go out. It affects the way we live, and some great social care movements have started here, with people who were changed by the message of Keswick. So it must be, but the devil's very subtle. What Jesus says here is not 'Either faith or works.' He's saying the devil can deceive you at both levels. There are some who talk and don't do, and there are some who do and don't believe. And your doing doesn't cover up your lack of knowledge of Jesus.

Was it not King Saul who disobeyed God's orders? But he made his sacrifice. Samuel had to say 'To obey is better than sacrifice.' Does not Paul remind us in 1 Corinthians 13, that you can have all the gifts of the Spirit; you can have the gift of knowledge, and you can speak in tongues, and you can prophesy, and you can be the kind of man whom people look to. What a mighty man! You can do signs and wonders – and if there's not love, it's nothing. Nothing at all. The Bible insists the devil knows how to do miracles. The magicians of Egypt could do miracles. It's not the mighty works that proclaim that you're right with God. It's your life that proclaims that you're right with God.

So I say to you tonight, it's more than doing. It depends on a relationship, and if you're in a relationship of love with somebody, you believe in them. And because you believe in them, you love them and you're not afraid to tell them that you love them. In the right sense, you worship them, and you'd do anything for them, but it springs out of love. And Jesus our Lord wants to say to you and me tonight, 'Philip, John, Mary – do you love me? Feed my sheep.' Is He Lord? 'No Entry.'

But just a thought about the 'One Way'. What is Jesus positively saying to us here, if it's more than believing and praising and doing? What does it mean to call Jesus Lord, to be able to say 'Your will be done' and mean it? Three simple things.

Discover God's will

Actually you don't have to look far to discover it. For example, it is always God's will that people should come to Christ. 'It is not the will of my Father that one of these little ones should perish,' said Jesus. He wills all men to be saved. So I know that it's God's will that I should be intent on the winning of people for Christ, because He's Lord. It's always His will that I should be holy; 1 Thessalonians 4:3, 'This is the will of God, even your holiness.' You don't have to pray whether or not the Lord wants you to break with that evil habit. There's nothing to pray about, He does and you know He does. And more than once, when people have come to me and said to me, 'I'll go away and pray about it,' I've said very rudely, 'No you won't – you'll go and do something about it.' There's nothing to pray about.

It is the will of God to be faithful in prayer. God forbid that I should sin against the Lord in ceasing to pray. If Jesus commands us, so we must do. We must pray – so I could go on and on, and in the particular avenue of your life, Jesus said, 'If you will to do My will, you shall know.' My guess is that for most of us, the problem about discovering God's will, is not that we can't find it, but that we daren't face it.

Secondly . . .

Do God's will

'He who does the will of my Father who is in heaven.' It's all a matter not of discussion, but of doing.

And thirdly . . .

Delight in God's will

When Jesus said, 'Not my will, but thine be done', it wasn't with passive resignation. It was with glad obedience – though it was costly. When Isaiah said, 'Here am I, send me,' it was the willing response of a joyful soul. God will force you into nothing.

I'm frightened of pressuring people. God doesn't. He lets you choose. And Isaiah heard not a command, but a question. 'Whom shall I send and who will go for us?' And he said, 'Here am I, send me.'

Do you delight to do God's will? In a way, oh, I hope it doesn't sound trite, it could be the best result of the preaching of God's Word tonight, if we go out with a joyful desire to do what we know we ought to do. In just the sheer joy of serving Him.

Oh, isn't it easy to forget it? He came down to Calvary. He said His 'I will', and He shed His blood and we just say 'I will' to Him.

I wonder if you can say it joyfully and audibly tonight. 'I will.' 'Jesus my Lord.' Then He won't say, 'Depart, I never knew you.' He'll say, 'Come, for I know you.' May it be true for every one of us, that we say, 'I will.'

RIVERS OF LIVING WATER

by Rev Michael Wilcock

John 7:38–39

Here in these few words we find the *picture* which our Lord is drawing of the Holy Spirit – 'rivers of living water'; the *promise* which He is making concerning the Holy Spirit – 'will flow out'; and the *person* our Lord describes as having the Holy Spirit – 'He who believes in Me, out of his innermost being will flow rivers of living water.' And I want to add to those three a fourth; a *process* which our Lord is implying with regard to the Holy Spirit.

The picture

First of all, then, the picture which our Lord paints. It's no surprise, in a book so full of pictures, that our Lord Jesus uses a picture to help us to grasp this very special truth. There is no way we can see the Holy Spirit. He is, in the nature of things, invisible; and so, says Jesus, 'Look at this picture.'

That pictorial river flows through the whole length of Scripture. It's there, right at the very beginning in Eden. And a river flows out of Eden, to water that garden, and it flows on through the books of the Bible, it flows through the history of God's people as God brings them into His promised land.

The river flows on into the book of Psalms and appears again and again as we read through those ancient Jewish songs. 'You visit the earth and water it, you greatly enrich it' – thus Psalm 65 speaks of the river of God, which I take it means the rain.

It's a river whose streams make glad the City of God. It's the river beside which the man of God finds himself flourishing (*cf.* Psa. 1:3, Jer. 17:7–8).

The river flows on in that magnificent vision that the prophet Ezekiel is given. And as it flows, so it broadens and deepens, and everything shall live where the river comes. 'And on its banks,' says Ezekiel (and this brings us echoes of the far end of Scripture), 'on both banks there grow all kinds of trees. There, fruit is to be for food and their leaves for healing.'

And that is what John, at the very end of the Bible, sees again. 'And there is the river, in all its eternal fullness, as it flows from the throne of God and of the Lamb, through the middle of the street of the city, and on either side of it the tree of life with its twelve kinds of fruit, and its leaves for the healing of the nation.'

It is a picture of a land which is fresh and green. All the other verses, that speak of the desert blossoming, and of the watered garden – they all speak to us of this picture. What is the picture meant to mean?

It is certainly a picture of what man wants. Here he finds his needs met, his problems solved, his emptiness filled. Here, particularly, he finds this thirst is quenched. As Jesus says, 'The man who is thirsty should come to Me. In Me is to be found that never-failing river.'

Now we've been warned in this convention of the peril of a preaching of the Word of God that focusses primarily on the needs of man. So perhaps it's better for us to think of this river supplying not so much what man wants (although it does do that), but to think of it supplying what God wants, because that is true also.

Follow the course of the river from Genesis to Revelation. Where does the river of Eden flow? It flows through a garden which is sinless. It waters the ground in the garden of God's perfection, as does its counterpart at the other end of Scripture, the river of paradise. How do we know that the river of Canaan is going to flow? Why, because God's people in the promised land, if they are wise, will recognise and obey the law of God and recognise, and be grateful for the grace of God. And where they turn to God, and God is the centre of their thoughts, there He says the river of God flows, and overflows. 'My blessing comes to those who seek what I want,' He said. And that is why the picture of the river is one of great fruitfulness.

I don't imagine that this landscape through which the river flows is any the less attractive because I say you can only have it on God's terms and not your terms. What God wants for you is even better than what you want for yourself. And if that river flows out through your life, you will find that what God wants is something greater and better than even you might desire for yourself. And God says, 'That is where My river will flow. It flows through My country, through My land, where My writ runs. If you belong in that country, then you will enjoy the benefits of that river.'

It is a marvellous picture, of the most desirable thing you can ever imagine. It is here, in and by that river, that all your needs are going to be met, and all your questions are going to be answered, and all you ills are going to be cured. You will find all possible refreshment and the quenching of every thirst and, above all, you will find fruitfulness in the service of the Lord Jesus. It is a river of living water, and this He said of the Spirit.

The Promise

What the promise means is that the power of the Spirit of God will flow out from the Christian to those around him. That is the great thing, and maybe the first thing you think of as you read this verse.

It flows out, in the first instance, to other Christians. Think of *the fruit of the Spirit*. Other people around you will be affected if you are producing the fruit of the Spirit, if there is love and joy and peace in your life, and long-suffering and gentleness and goodness. If there is faithfulness, meekness and self-control and all these flow out from you to the folk around, they will be blessed as God's Holy Spirit blesses you.

The result will be another great New Testament word, *the fellowship of the Spirit*. You'll find that you're bound together as the Spirit flows out from you to them, and from them back to you. And you'll find that that kind of fellowship overcomes all sorts of natural barriers, and brings together people who normally wouldn't mix.

But we find, as the river flows out from me to you, and from you to me, *the unity of the Spirit* – a third great New Testament phrase.

This is what the Spirit is doing – producing fruit, creating fellowship, creating unity. And this is the promise of our Lord, that the rivers of living water will flow out. And then they will flow out beyond us.

It's a great thing to belong to a community of Christian people in which the power of the Spirit spreads to and fro in this way, but the Lord intends that it shall spread further than that. The Spirit will flow out into the unbelieving world around the church. This river will convict the world of sin and righteousness and judgement as it flows out. And how will it do that? 'Why,' says Jesus, 'As the Father sent

Me, so I send you. He gave Me the Spirit in fullness, and so He will do to you.'

And having said that, He breathed on them and said, 'Receive the Holy Spirit.' It is in that power that you go out from the church into the world, and the Spirit will flow out, a river of living water into the unbelieving world around you. And so it is.

As we pass on from the Gospels into the book of Acts, we find the Lord Jesus promising that His people will first be baptised in the Holy Spirit, and will then go out to witness in the power of the Holy Spirit. When the church prays, the Holy Spirit says, 'Separate Me Barnabas and Saul, to the work to which I have called them.' And so He says, all down history.

It is the Spirit who directs, because the Spirit is flowing out through His people, into the world that needs His message. 'I promise I'll do it.' says Jesus. 'He who believes in Me, out of his innermost being shall flow the rivers of living water. And this He said of the Spirit.' And where that river flows, everything will live. That too, is a promise, and it will happen.

I wonder what your reaction is to all that? I suppose it's very possible that when I speak in these terms, concerning this wonderful picture of the Holy Spirit and the fact that it is the promise of the Lord that the river will flow out of you, that your reaction is: 'I wish it did! I see all too little of it. Why should that be?'

And so we're left with the question as to why we think the promise doesn't come true. But I have to say to you again, that the Lord Jesus says, 'He who believes in Me, out of his innermost being, will flow the rivers of living water', meaning the Spirit.

The Person

Jesus speaks of the person who has the Spirit. 'He who believes.' Now we need to be clear about what our Lord is saying here, because some believers would say that their experience doesn't measure up to what they were led to believe might happen, when the Spirit took hold of them.

We ask ourselves questions about that kind of disappointment. 'Why don't I experience what I think Jesus is talking about here? Is it a question of how I believe? Well, perhaps I'm not believing properly. I feel so dry. I wonder if there is such a thing as the river of the water of life. Is it because I'm not believing hard or sincerely or fervently enough?' I'm sure there are many Christians who get hung up on this kind of question.

But as soon as you begin to think along that line, you must realise that the kind of faith you're talking about is contrary to what the Bible tells us faith is. The moment you start talking about how you're going to believe – that's exactly what believing is not. Believing means something that *you* don't do. It means that I say, 'Lord, You've done it, – that's what I rest on.' If I ask, 'Am I believing wrongly?', I'm asking the wrong kind of question.

'Well, perhaps it's not a question of how I believe, but a question of whom or what? Whom should I believe?'

But, you know, as soon as you say, 'Is it a question of whom or what?', you have the answer right here. Jesus says this experience is for him who believes 'in Me' – that's all. Not believing any particular doctrine. Not even believing in the Holy Spirit. Do you believe in Jesus? That's what Jesus says.

'Well,' you say, 'I still don't quite understand it. Is it a question of when? Because I notice here that it says that he who believes in Me, out of his heart shall flow the river. Perhaps it's a case of something I've got to wait for, until

I'm more mature as a Christian, till I understand a bit more, till I've had a further revelation from God about it, till I've had a second blessing equivalent to my original new birth.'

If you read on to the next verse you will see why Jesus said he who believes will find this to be true. The reason it was still a future experience for them was simply that the Spirit had not been given and Jesus had not yet been glorified.

But now Jesus has been glorified, and He has sent down the Holy Spirit, and there's no more 'will' about it. It's a present thing. All you have to do is put your trust in Jesus, and you have the river of living water flowing out from your heart. Your experience may say, 'I don't quite go along with that,' but the Word of God says, 'He who believes in Jesus has the Spirit flowing out from him.' 'Ah, but,' you say, 'That simply sharpens up the question. It simply makes me ask all the more, "How come that I don't experience what I think I ought to experience?"'

The Process

So I want to bring you lastly what seems to me to be a process which our Lord implies, concerning the Holy Spirit. 'He who believes in Me, as the Scripture has said, out of his innermost being will flow rivers of living water'. I want you to notice particularly that our Lord Jesus does not say, 'Out of him will flow the river.' He says, 'Out of his heart, out of his innermost being, out of the core of his personality will flow the rivers of living water.' It's as if when you and I were born again, God set, in the inmost core of our being, a spring of unquenchable water, which is the Spirit of God, there at the central point of your personality and mine. And before there can be any outflow from me to my fellow Christians, let alone from me to the world around, the river of living water has to flow from my innermost core, out into the rest of me. I need to be filled with the Holy Spirit.

The Holy Spirit has been given to me by my Father in heaven when I was born again, in order to convict me first. To teach me, before He teaches the rest, to re-fashion me, to empower, not simply the church, but me. The Holy Spirit is here to sanctify – that's why He's called the Holy Spirit – and as He flows out from my innermost being He is set to fill me, and to make me like Jesus, and then to flow out through me to the folk around. And if there is no outflowing from me to the fellowship of Christians around me, or to the world beyond that, it may just be that I'm hindering that flow within myself.

The Bible has plenty to say about the Spirit being grieved, about Him being quenched; or perhaps if you think that quenching is not the right picture to go with a river, perhaps we ought to think of the river being dammed up, blocked off. There are all sort of ways in which I may hinder the power of the Holy Spirit, which is there, which has within itself the power of flowing out – actually from flowing out into my mind, and my eyes, and my fingers and my feet – the way I walk, the way I think, the way I act. And I am preventing that.

But He's there. When I pray, 'Spirit of the living God, fall afresh on me, break me, melt me, mould me, fill me,' that is a good prayer. But perhaps I ought to be thinking rather, 'Spirit of the living God, enable me, quite deliberately, to start obeying You, where I know I ought to be obedient. To start tailoring my life to You, the way I know I should. Actually to allow myself to be led by You. Actually, in practice, moment by moment, to permit You to conform me to the image of my Saviour.'

I am quite sure that if we were to let the Spirit of God flow out into every moment of our day, every thought of our mind, every action of our life, then of course we would overflow. We couldn't help but do so, and flow on out into the world around. May that be so in our experience!

HEAVEN FINDS A PLACE FOR A PENITENT HEART

by Rev Gordon Bridger

Psalm 51

Psalm 51 shows us David's way back to God out of a deep sense of guilt. He is the prodigal returning to his father, the penitent coming back to God. And we may feel that we are in a very similar situation, and God has spoken directly to us about a very similar sin.

Or it may be simply that as we came under the ministry of God's Word, we found God the Spirit touching upon other areas of our lives where we know there is sin to be confessed, where we know there's something to put right, and where we began to feel that probing of the Spirit of God in our own conscience. And we want to be the kind of people God wants us to be, but we know that this sin in our lives can hinder that.

So what is the way back to God? How do we deal with sin of this kind?

I want to suggest from Psalm 51 four things that may help us.

Don't cover up

There had been all that cover up, but David came through to that point as Nathan spoke to him the word of the Lord, when he acknowledged his sin. 'I have sinned against the Lord.' And that's the first step back, isn't it always? Honestly, openly to acknowledge my sin before the Lord. He accepted responsibility for it.

Accept responsibility for sin

That's the first thing I want to say under this heading. He accepted responsibility for his sin. 'Have mercy on me, my transgressions, my sin is ever before me.' I think that many of us find it difficult, right from our early days, to acknowledge sin. We tend to try to project our faults upon other people.

I remember when one of my daughters was very young, about two and a half to three years of age. Sometimes she would be doing something just a little naughty, like, for instance, taking some sweets out of a cupboard and eating them behind the sofa. And when I came into the room, as soon as I saw her and was obviously about to say something to her, she would get in first with something like, 'Naughty naughty Daddy, Daddy is horrid.' Now, Daddy is naughty and horrid. He was then, and still is at times – but so was she!

But right from the beginning (because, as David says here, we have inherited this sinful nature of Adam), we don't like to acknowledge our own sins; we project our own sin and failure so often on other people. I think too, there is a trend today in some Christian circles, to blame not others, but to blame the devil for all our sins and failures. Now we are not ignorant of his devices, we know how powerful he is, we know how much he was behind the temptation of David and our temptations. But I think there is a danger when we say too easily, 'What I need to be delivered from is this spirit of pride, or laziness, or conceit,' rather than, 'I need to repent of my pride, my deceit, my laziness.' David acknowledged his sins, he faced up to that responsibility.

I suppose the other thing is that quite honestly, some-times we just don't notice our own sin. We see the faults in others. You remember how Jesus put it so humorously? We've got a wacking great plank in our own eye, but we see the speck in other people's eyes. We don't seem to be aware of our own sin at all.

And we find it incredibly easy to see the faults in others; it rarely occurs to us that there is any real fault in ourselves. But David acknowledged his sins. 'Have mercy on me, O my God. I know my transgressions. My sin is ever before me.' And that's the first step. No cover-up, accept responsi-bility for our sin.

Secondly . . .

Acknowledge the seriousness of sin

Don't cover that up either. David calls sins 'transgression' in verses 1, 3, and 13. It means rebellion, defiance against God; breaking His law in deliberate defiance. And David had come to see that that was what sin was. He had broken God's law, he had defied God. It's important to recognise that and sin for what it really is.

You may remember in James Dobson's books about bringing up children, he encourages parents, when trying to discipline their children, to see the distinction between wil-ful defiance and childish irresponsibility. That's an impor-tant point. But if you're a parent, you'll remember, and if you've young children, you'll know that from the earliest days, wilful defiance is there.

I shall never forget when I spoke rather strongly to another of my daughters, when she was about two and a half. I said, 'Mary, do this!' I forget what particular thing it was, but it was clearly something I felt ought to be a com-mand and that she should obey. And I can see her now, with her face red and her lips trembling, standing up to me, looking up into my face and saying, 'By the hair of my chinny chin chin, I won't.' Well, those of you who are literary scholars will know the allusion. And of course we laugh and we smile, don't we, at childish defiance.

But you see that David is saying, 'I recognise that now. And I don't plead that I was born with a twist in my nature, I don't say that I am not responsible.' Indeed he says in his early verses, 'Against You, You only God, have I sinned – I deserve nothing,' he says, 'but Your judgement. I have rebelled against You. I have defied Your laws, I have broken Your laws.' And David says to us, 'No cover up'; he acknowledged responsibility for his sin. He acknowledged the seriousness of his sin; it was transgression.

It was also iniquity, which was a word from verse 5, meaning 'falling short of God's standards.' Failing God, and not only God, he had failed Bathsheba, Uriah, the unnamed child, Nathan, the people of God, but above all, he saw that the seriousness of sin was in grieving God, in failing God, in letting God down, in hurting God.

'Adultery,' says Paul, 'is a sin against our own bodies.' That is what makes it particularly serious. But it is also, and primarily, a sin against God. If we ever forget the seriousness of sin we need to look at the cross. You know the *spiritual*, 'Were you there when they crucified my Lord?' Sin is my responsibility. When I sin, I must acknowledge that sin is serious, and when I sin, it is primarily a sin against God, even though it is also a sin against others. And the first step back to God is not to cover up my sin, but to acknowledge it.

Don't give up

'Don't give up,' says David. That is, don't give up hoping in the mercy and forgiveness of God.

As I read this Psalm again, it seemed to me that there were two particularly lovely truths about the love of God, as David reflects on his own experience of forgiveness.

First there's the thought of God's commitment to us. 'Have mercy on me, O God,' he says in verse 1, 'according to your steadfast love.' And all the commentators tell us that the Hebrew word translated in that way, is the word for a covenant. For God covenanting Himself to us, committing Himself to us in love. It's the kind of word we might use of a bride and bridegroom covenanting together at the start of their married life.

I shall never forget hearing a story a few years ago of a husband and wife, who for many years lived happily together and were a loving married couple. And then the husband was unfaithful to his wife. But he was deeply sorry for what he'd done, returned and asked for her forgiveness. Seeing the genuineness of his repentance, and because she had committed herself to him for life, she forgave him and accepted him back. But it was not without cost. Her hair went prematurely white as a result of the shock of that unfaithfulness. Their marriage was rebuilt. She was able to accept him back, but not without cost.

David, when he speaks of God's steadfast, covenant love, helps us to look forward to that time when Jesus said, 'This is the cup of the New Covenant in my blood which is shed for you and for many, for the forgiveness of sins.' Jesus has committed Himself to us, but not without cost. On the cross He bore our sin; on the cross He became a curse for us, that He might redeem us from the curse and condemnation of the law. But He loves us like that, with a steadfast love, and a covenant love, sealed on the cross.

David experienced something of that, and something of the completeness of God's forgiveness. There are a number of lovely pictures in Psalm 51, which help us to see just how complete the forgiveness is that was offered to David.

Look, for example, at verse 2 – the idea of cleansing. Or verse 7 – 'Purge me with hyssop.' This is the picture of the leper or someone with some kind of skin disease, who was regarded as defiled and, therefore, cut off from the people of God. When the skin disease was cured he went to the priest. The priest would get blood from the altar, from the sacrifice, and he would sprinkle him with blood as a symbol of saying, 'Through this sacrifice your defilement has been removed. You can once again return and meet with your people.'

David felt something of that defilement. And you know, unconfessed sin has that effect, hasn't it? We can't look our friends in the face; we don't like to see the vicar. But the forgiveness God offers is that which wipes that away, cleanses the defilement that sin brings to us.

There is another picture, in verses 2 and 7 and that is a slightly different one. The picture here seems to be the washing of clothes which have a deep stain in them. John Goldingay, in his commentary, says it's rather like washing nappies. And what David is trying to say to us here is that God was offering him a forgiveness and a cleansing that could remove the deepest stain. Whatever you've done in the past and however much you feel it's stained your life, God's complete forgiveness is such that He can remove every stain. 'Wash me, and I shall be whiter than snow,' says David.

And the third picture, verse 9, is of being wiped clean. It's like wiping the slate clean. Some of you may remember those slates. Children could scribble on them and then it was clean. That's the picture.

Do you see what that means? God not only forgives when we confess our sin and turn to Him in repentance, but He gives us a completely new start. He wipes the slate clean. Indeed, you remember how he says, 'God will remember your sins no more.' We feel like saying sometimes, 'But Lord, can you forgive again that sin? I only committed that last week.' And God will say 'What sin, what sin? If you confessed it to me I remember it no more. I blot it out. I wiped the slate clean. I give you a totally new start.' And David knew something of that. How much more, in the light of the cross, should we!

Don't dry up

By this I mean that forgiveness on its own is not enough. I also need renewal. I need to know something of that experience when I've sinned and come and confessed my sins and know that God has forgiven my sins. I need to know something of that renewing work of what Jesus calls 'the rivers of living water' flowing from within, purifying and bubbling out again. So that something of that joy which I've lost and that power that I've lost, returns. David teaches us the importance of that in verses 10 and onwards. 'Cast me not away from thy presence, and take not thy Holy Spirit from me.'

In the Old Testament, often the Holy Spirit comes upon someone for a particular task. David had seen Saul with the Spirit removed from him – powerless, ineffective. 'I don't want that experience. I want Your Spirit to return to me.' Now for us, born again of the Spirit of God, the Spirit is within us, but we can quench Him, we can resist Him, we can grieve Him. And we need to pray, 'Restore to me the joy of your salvation and uphold me with a willing spirit.'

If you were to go more deeply than we have time tonight into that passage, you would see, I think, reading between the lines, something of what David experienced when he was unrenewed, when his sin was not forgiven. I think he must have felt very dirty, because he prays for cleanliness, and when you've sinned and you've not put it right, that's exactly how we feel.

I think he must have often felt dispirited. He says in verse 8, 'Fill me with joy and gladness; let the bones which you have broken rejoice.' Or it might be, 'Let me hear joy and gladness.' Because even when he went into church, into the temple to worship, covering up the things that he'd done and not put right, there was no joy in his heart. You know that experience, I know it, when things are not right. And worship had become a duty only, and not a joy. Christian service had become a drudgery. And so he prays for that renewing of the Spirit and that upholding of the Spirit which will enable him to be more effective.

And so he says, in verse 13, 'I've neglected this work of telling others but my tongue, when I'm renewed and for-given, will sing aloud of your deliverance.'

You see, true penitence includes renewal, the renewing of the Spirit of God. C.S. Lewis once said of Christians,

> The egg can do one of two things. It can hatch out and become a chicken, presumably an uncomfortable thing for an egg, or it can gradually go bad. The one thing it can't do is remain a decent, respectable egg.

Even when you've asked for the forgiveness of God, what you and I need at that point is the renewing of the Spirit of God. We need Him to create a clean heart in us, to put a new and right spirit within us. We need to be upheld with His Spirit so that we can go back into His work with joy. We need to have the joy of our salvation given back to us.

Don't opt out

That's the force, the point of asking, acknowledging his sin, asking for forgiveness, praying for renewal, believing that God would give it. And then he realised that what that meant was that he could go back into the temple of God.

Before, when he had offered sacrifices with an unrenewed, unforgiven, uncleansed heart, God could not hear him. But now, because he has a broken and a contrite heart, he knows God will not despise him. So he returns into the house of God to do what he couldn't do himself. To open his mouth to praise Him from a humble heart.

And then verses 18 and 19. Some people believe that's added later, that this was, as it were, the church perhaps in the time of the captivity saying, 'We identify with David . . . Now in the light of what we learnt from David's experience, let's get back to the work we've got to do. Let's put right the things that are wrong.'

And true repentance is always like that. We not only return to the house of God with renewed praise, but we return to the work of God with renewed confidence. We start to build the walls of that relationship, of our family life, of the disagreements in our church, of the broken walls of our ministry. We're involved, we don't opt out. We opt in.

So may I say as I close, if God has been speaking to you; may I say again, don't cover up. Tell Him about it. Don't give up, trust in God's complete mercy. He loves you and gave Himself for you. Don't dry up, let Him come and fill your life by His Spirit. Let Him renew you and restore to you that joy and that effectiveness that you've lost. And don't opt out, but tell Him you'll go back to that situation and work for Him and serve Him all the days of your life.

TWO CONVICTIONS, TWO RESPONSES

by Rev David Jackman

2 Corinthians 5:15

At the root of the 'sin problem', lies the 'self problem'; for at root, all sin is an assertion of myself against God. The heart of sin is an attack upon His perfect love. For every time I disobey Him or ignore Him, I am saying He doesn't really love me, He isn't really working for my good. It's a denial of His attributes of perfect wisdom and righteousness. Every time I sin, I am saying I know better than God. I run my life my way, and as a teenager once wrote in an essay that I had to mark: 'Even though I may make a mess of it, at least it will be my own mess.'

Deep within us all there is the problem of self-will, that disobeys God's commandments; the problem of self-pity, that poisons so many Christian lives; the problem of self-sufficiency that thinks, I can go it alone without God; and the problem of self-centredness. Me at the heart of my world.

There is only one solution radical enough to deal with that problem, and that solution is death. There is a song that we sometimes sing these days that says,

> Jesus take me as I am,
> I can come no other way.
> Lead me deeper into you,
> Make my flesh-life melt away.

But it doesn't melt away! The only solution to the problem of self is the radical solution of death, and there is only one death that has that sort of power – the death that happened at Calvary.

We so often leave the cross out of the reckoning. We rush to verse 17. We long to live in the joy and fulfilment of that new creation. Quite rightly so, for it is every Christian's birthright. But we forget verse 17 begins with 'therefore', and that the 'therefore' takes us back to the Calvary event in verse 14, on which all our Christian experience depends. It is because He died for all, that the new creation has come.

This is the event which has tranformed everything. The place where the old things passed away and where the new came was Calvary, and He died so that all those who live should no longer live for themselves, but for Him who died for them, and was raised again.

So Paul is saying to us, the crucial moment in human history, where everything was changed between God and us, was the moment when His Son gave Himself up for us all. I want to unpack something of what the Holy Spirit is saying through Paul in these few verses.

Let me suggest to you that there are two convictions about the cross, that we need to hold and two responses to the resurrection that we need to make.

Two convictions about the cross

Firstly the two convictions. They are both very basic, but they are absolutely essential, if you and I are to grow in our

knowledge and love of God. The first is there, in verse 14.
Let's read it as if we have never heard it before. *One died
for all*. Christ died for us all. Now, we are not theorising
about some mystical initiation into the divine life of a universal spirit. We are set in a clear position historically, by
what Paul is saying. A man died. The God-man died, and in
that death, the Lord Jesus Christ did something that
changed the whole of human history, and potentially
changed your life and mine, in terms of our relationship
with God. That mighty event reaches down through history
and encompasses the whole world, the world that God
made, the world that He has kept on loving, the world for
which He gave His Son. 'One died for all.'

Well, of course, Paul is not teaching a universalism that
says everyone is reconciled to God automatically, through
the work of Christ. If he were doing that, he would be saying that the evangelist's task is simply that of telling all men
that they are reconciled to God, whether they like it or not.
I know that there are some who teach that. But it isn't what
the New Testament teaches. In fact, it would make nonsense of the biblical doctrine of human responsibility,
which is, in fact, the root of Paul's appeal in this very chapter.

If you look down the page to verse 20, you will see that he
makes his appeal on behalf of God. And he says not 'Recognise that you are already reconciled', but 'Be reconciled'.
Turn to God, trust Him.

He is writing to Christians to whom that is already a reality, but when we go out into the world and speak to those
who do not know, we call upon them as Jesus did, to repent
and to believe the good news.

The idea of Christ dying for us and for all, is the doctrine
of Christ as our representative, and our substitute, which is
central to biblical thinking about the cross. As often is the
case, one of our hymns puts it very clearly, when it says

> Bearing shame and scoffing rude,
> In my place condemned He stood.
> Sealed my pardon with His blood.
> Hallelujah, what a Saviour!

Because the most amazing thing in all the world, is the cross of Jesus Christ.

Now, the 'all for whom he died' are those who see in the death of Christ their representative dying in their place, their substitute dying for their sins, and who gladly identify with Him by faith.

Do you remember how Martin Luther is said to have defined faith? He said, 'Faith is saying "Yes, this is for me".' And when you see that you are included in those for whom Christ died, when you can say from your heart, 'He did it for me', you begin to deal with the self-problem at the root of the sin-problem.

This principle God taught His Old Testament people, of course, at the Passover. In every household there occurred a death. Either the Passover lamb died for that household, or the first-born son in the household died. Either the family sheltered under the blood of the lamb spread on the doorpost and the lintels, or the angel of death demanded the life of the first-born. And what God was teaching there, He is continually underlining in our lives. The price which sin demands must be paid, either through the death of the Lamb of God, or by my own eternal separation from God.

So this is where we all need to start, by seeing that Jesus died for us, that we are included in the atoning work; that by repentance and by faith in what He has done, it is possible for us to enter into the free forgiveness of the children of God. And when you are overwhelmed by the love of Christ on the cross and you take that first step on the way of discipleship, you can say, 'He died for me.'

But the second conviction that follows in verse 14, is *and therefore all died*. The 'all' for whom He died are the 'all who have died in Christ's death'. That's why the tense is so clear there; it's a once-for-all action.

Now, there are these two levels of our understanding, aren't there. There is the level that we've just thought about, that says Christ's death was my death in that He died in my place. So when Jesus died, I died because He was doing it for me (verse 21).

But there is a second deeper level in which I died in Christ, for His death was not only a death for sin, it was a death to sin. Christ died not only so that I might live, but as verse 15 says, that I might live a resurrection life. That means life beyond death, a life that is lived no longer for myself but for Him.

Therefore, it is true to say that Christ died so that I might die. When Jesus said to His disciples, 'You shall indeed drink of my cup,' that was what He was saying, but for us, it is a cup of blessing. For us it is the means by which the problem of ourselves and of the flesh is dealt with. It is the means by which we die to ourselves in order to live a new life in God.

So Paul, in the final letter to the Corinthians, 'The cup of blessing which we bless, is it not a participation in the blood of Christ?' And I want you to notice with me, the inclusiveness and the certainty of it all; all died. It is the final unconditional event.

As far as a Christian is concerned, it has already happened. For in the death of Jesus there is the total victory over all the hostile forces that are ranged against me, the sin that would condemn me, the flesh that would ensnare me, the world that would divert me. He put the principalities of that old order to flight as He hung there in triumph on the cross, so that they have no power over Jesus, and they have no power over those who are in Christ.

This is the new creation of which we are a part by God's grace and through faith, and it is only by faith that this reality can become ours in practical experience. That is why, in a parallel passage well known to many of us, in Romans 6:11, Paul says, 'Therefore count yourself dead to sin but alive to God'.

Consider it to be so, because it is so. The call to faith is a call to identify ourselves with these convictions about the cross. That is what faith is.

We do not necessarily have to feel them emotionally for them to be the reality that grounds us in our Christian lives. We have by faith to reckon on them and to live on that foundation. Some of us make the mistake of trying to 'feel' the cross. Now there are times in which we will feel the love of Christ, in which we will feel deep sorrow for our sin, in which we will sense what Jesus suffered there; but what we have got to do day by day is to reckon on what He has done for us and to identify ourselves with these convictions. A Christian life is the affirmation of that fact.

I can only do that in faith and in hope. That is how I assume my radical new identity. By faith, I believe that on the cross the Lord Jesus Christ destroyed the power of sin in my life and re-established a new creation. By faith, I identify myself with that new order, and my hope is for the full realisation of that new order of life increasingly, in this world, and perfectly in His presence, so that the old self is nailed to the cross.

Now, in experience, I find that old self often clamouring for recognition, so every day I have to look that sin-soaked self full in the face and refuse to recognise it as the real me. That is not my true identity before God. That old self is crucified, and is not what I shall one day be in the presence of Christ.

When we claim to be Christians, we are claiming that our real selves are defined by Christ's victory over all the hostile powers that would otherwise destroy us. Do you have that conviction about the cross? Can you say, not only Jesus died for me, but I died with Him?

Two responses to the resurrection

The resurrection in the work of salvation is Paul's focus at the end of verse 15. Let's look very briefly at the two responses to the resurrection that that verse encourages us to make.

The cross and the resurrection, are so closely bound together in apostolic thinking because they are so closely bound together in Christian experience. If I know that my old self has been dealt with by the cross, and if I am living in the daily experience of that by faith, then my new self is being energised and empowered by the resurrection. And the characteristic of someone who is living that way is that *we no longer live for ourselves* (*cf.* verse 15).

There is a sense in which sin robbed us of our humanity, and in which redemption is a work that restores and reconstitutes man as man. Sanctification, or becoming like Christ, is then a progress towards a true humanity. The true self is the new creation in Christ, which we have seen in verse 17, and the process of growth in the Christian life is that gradual change from a sub-human parody to a true integrated humanity.

We draw on the life of Christ, so that there is a sense in which it is true to say that being a Christian is becoming a real human being born the first time. That's why the theologians called the Lord Jesus Christ 'The proper man', because there is a sense in which there is only one true man that the world has ever seen.

If the life of the risen Christ is planted within us, our privilege is to live for Him and not for ourselves. That means that we shall experience the sort of new motivation that Paul talks about in verse 14, where he says at the start of the verse, 'Christ's love compels us!' That is, the inner dynamic which brings about the radical change at the heart of things for a Christian. The motivating power is not my love for Him, but His love for me.

It is a very interesting verb, that verb 'compels'. It means at root, 'to hold things together', and so it came to be used to express the idea of pressing hard, squeezing something together – used in the Gospels about the crowd pressing on the Lord Jesus. It is used in secular Greek about besieging a city. To me, the modern equivalent is being on the Northern Line in a rush hour. He says Christ's love is like that, because the resurrection power of Jesus is in me, and I am so absorbed and occupied by Christ's love for me, and my desire to love Him, that that has redirected all my thoughts and energies. I no longer live for myself. I am restrained and compelled by the love of Calvary. It is an internal pressure that changes our lives from the inside out.

That is why Paul did not live for himself. He had found someone better to live for. As Malcolm Muggeridge puts it, 'He had been liberated from the tiny citadel of our inflated ego!' Has Christ set you free from living for yourself? That is what being a Christian is all about.

So he had a new attitude to other people, as a result. 'Once we regarded Christ from a worldly point of view, but now we regard no one from that point of view' (*cf.* verse 16). It was true of his attitude to others as well as his attitude to the Lord. The worldy point of view says, 'I will judge everything from my reference point.' But that old self had gone; and the new self was in the power of the risen Christ, so a Christian is someone who knows that people are no longer there to be used.

He is not asking the question, 'What do I get out of this?' He is asking the question, 'How can I share Christ's love and life with them?' They are no longer there to be feared. They are there to be prayed for, and cared for. He is no longer living for himself, not concerned about getting but giving, because the opposite of the love of Christ is not hatred, it is self-love.

It is self-love that kills so many human relationships. But Paul says that if we are living for Christ, we do not look at people from a worldly standpoint any longer, we look at them with His eyes. And His love within us re-directs our energies so that we are 'giving' people, who long to be a blessing wherever God takes us. One response to the resurrection; no longer live for myself.

Look at the second one that is linked to it in verse 15. 'But for him.' *We live for him.* I wonder if that is really true of our lives before God tonight. It is so very easy for those of us who have been Christians for some time to live for our church, to live for our ministry, for our service, perhaps even to live for evangelism, but Paul says, 'No, I live for Him.' Only Jesus is central. And if you are not living for Him, you are an eccentric Christian. We have to be Christ-centred.

That is the only way our lives will work properly anyway, when Christ is the hub, when He is the focus, when He is the goal. That's why, you see, we are not to be in a constant quest for an 'it', for something that will make me a super-saint, grade-one Christian, because if I could find an 'it' that would do that, what would be at the centre of my life? *I* would be. We have been made new creations so *He* may be at the centre of our lives, and so that we might live for Him.

How are we doing it? Start by praising Him. Do you walk through the day praising the Lord Jesus? Go on by pleasing Him, responding to His Word in obedience, thinking how can I show Him how much I love Him. How can I allow His risen power to flow through me more fully? That's why Jesus died and was raised again; so that we should no longer live for ourselves but for Him, so that every moment should count for Him. That is why He died and that is why He rose.

No wonder Paul says in verse 13, 'If we are out of our mind, it is for the sake of God.' If you think that is extreme and eccentric, well, Paul says, 'I am doing it for the sake of God. For Christ's love compels us, because we are convinced that Jesus died for us and therefore we died in him' – that old self has been taken away. It is not our true identity. We are new creatures in Christ. He has done that for us through His death and resurrection, so that we should no longer live for ourselves but for Him. That's the potential. Faith and obedience make it actual.

THE LORDSHIP OF CHRIST
by Dr Stephen Olford

Romans 12:1–2

A life of surrender

There is only one true response to the lordship of Christ, and that is total surrender. As we have heard so clearly tonight, Jesus Christ is Lord. The question is, how do we respond? How do we answer that challenge of His lordship?

I know no verses in any part of the Bible that help me to understand that so much as these first two verses of Romans 12. I want you to look with me first, at God's plea for a life of surrender. That word 'I beseech you' means 'I call you alongside of me, I beseech you, I plead with you'. It's an amazing statement. Of course, Paul is writing the letter, but he is using the very voice of the Spirit of God Himself, of Jesus Christ his Lord, and he says, 'I beseech you by the mercies of God that you present your bodies a living sacrifice.' What is the basis of this plea? It moves me profoundly as I think of it.

The basis is that little phrase, 'The mercies of God'. The mercies of God, as revealed of course, in the Lord Jesus Christ as Lord and Saviour. The revelation of His love.

That's why he bursts into that tremendous doxology in 11:33–36.

What are these mercies of God? The unfolding of His wisdom, and the knowledge that God has stepped into human history in the person of the Lord Jesus Christ and poured out His life in order to redeem and justify and sanctify and glorify men who are shut up in the prison house of sin, condemned without exception, without excuse, as we find in the early chapters of this epistle. And in the light of that amazing revelation of His love, He says, 'I beseech you, present your bodies, a living sacrifice, holy, acceptable unto God.' Not only the revelation of His love, but the expectation of His love. Look at the closing sentence of verse 1; 'which is your reasonable service', or your spiritual mode of worship and response.

Love truly appreciated must be reciprocated. The greatest sin in the universe is unrequited love, and if I know what God has done for me in Jesus Christ, if the cross of the Lord Jesus Christ means anything to me, then I cannot but say; 'Love so amazing, so divine, demands my soul, my life, my all.' If these divine mercies do not move me to that kind of response, nothing in the world ever will.

This was what broke my heart as a young man of twenty-one. I was brought up on the mission field and saved at a very young age. But it wasn't until the age of twenty-one, on a virtual death-bed, that God broke my heart with a vision of the cross. That's why I have an empathy with that moment in John Calvin's life, when having written theology, having demonstrated the wisdom and power of his intellect, he was broken. And he looked into the face of his Lord and he made that amazing statement which he had inscribed on his coat-of-arms – 'If Jesus Christ be God as He said it and died for me, then I have to respond.' And the words he formulated were these: 'Lord Jesus I give thee everything, I keep back nothing for myself.'

But this text teaches something which I feel is terribly important in a Keswick Convention. It's what I'm going to call, 'God's pattern for a life of surrender.' I want you to look at these words very carefully; 'I beseech you therefore, brethren, by the mercies of God, that you present [or yield] your bodies a living sacrifice, holy, acceptable to God.' How am I to respond to this unbelievable, overwhelming love? The love which makes Paul cry out, 'Oh the riches of the wisdom and knowledge of God,' this wisdom in Christ who has been made unto us righteousness, sanctification and redemption – how do I respond?

Yieldingly

First of all, yieldingly. 'Present' – that word means an act followed by an attitude. A once-for-all act that carries ramifications and implications all through the rest of my life. It means bringing my entire life, unreservedly, totally. The word has roots in the Old Testament. In the Greek Old Testament, it is used for a gift being handed over. You don't hand over a gift and take it back again. That's the meaning too, of those wonderful faculties that God has given us. Everything in us, your bodies, your faculties, not one of them is to be left off the altar of God's acceptance. It's the picture of Old Testament times, when that bullock was brought to the north side of the altar and slain and flayed, and then cut into its portions as God prescribed. Every piece of that bullock, every piece put onto that brazen altar, deliberately, thoughtfully and totally. The Bible teaches that God never consecrates a part, He only consecrates the whole. If your life is going to be the burnt offering of this verse, then it must be totally, totally yielded.

I know of no hymn to equal that of Frances Ridley

Havergal, in which she goes right through from the head to the foot of her personality, and each piece as it were is laid upon the altar: 'Take my life, take my moments, take my hands, take my mind, take my voice, take my silver, take my gold, take my will, take my heart, take myself, I will be ever, only, all for thee.' Have you laid every area of your life, every faculty of your life, upon the altar of God's acceptance?

It's not without significance that these two verses move right into all the gifts, or some of the gifts as some people like to put them. I don't know what gift or gifts you may have, but every Christian has a gift. Are you prepared to bring everything, *everything*, and lay it upon the altar with utter yieldingness?

Livingly

It means that you are going to bring that life of yours intelligently. You are not going to come like a dumb animal or a bird. That bullock, that goat, that dove didn't know what was going to happen. But you are to bring your life intelligently; your mind matters. You are going to say 'Yes Lord, I want my mind, my eyes, my lips, my hands. I know what I'm doing, I'm doing it intelligently.'

Spiritually alive

It means that you recognise that you've been quickened by the Spirit in regeneration and that you as a born-again Christian are yielding your life. But it means more than that. The reference here is way back to chapter 6. 'Yield yourselves as those that are alive from the dead' – those who have accepted the sentence of the cross upon their self-life, and continue to accept that sentence upon the cross, so that self, self is on the cross, Christ is on the throne. And in that union of life with Christ, you reckon yourself to be dead to sin but alive unto God through Jesus Christ our Lord, and that's the life you bring upon the altar and say, 'Lord, this is the life I want you to use.'

Continually alive

But it means something more. Not only intelligently alive, not only spiritually alive, but continually alive. It's a reference actually to the Old Testament sacrifices that were placed upon that brazen altar, and when every piece was put upon that altar, the job wasn't done. The priest had to stay there, and he had two instruments at least, known in the Old Testament as flesh-hooks. And those flesh-hooks were placed upon that sacrifice and that sacrifice was kept at the centre of that flame. Many a time those big sacrifices tended to slip off from the altar, but back they came, again, and again, and again, until the sacrifice was wholly consumed. You can name those flesh-hooks what you will. For me they mean two things; determination and discipline.

Determination – why? Because determination is more than desire. My father, who was a missionary for thirty-five years in the heart of Africa, used to say, 'Determination, not desire controls my destiny.' Are you determined to be a totally yielded Christian? Well, put that flesh-hook in.

Discipline. I believe that's the other flesh-hook. How do I demonstrate that I am truly yielded? By getting up and having my quiet time; not because I feel like it, but because it's the right thing to do. By coming to the prayer meeting. Why? Because it's the right thing to do. By having fellowship with God's people. Why? Because it's the right thing to do. By reading my Bible. Why? Because it's the right thing to do. By going out in evangelism. Why? Because it's the right thing to do. And that calls for discipline.

The Bible teaches both 'the rest of faith', and the striving to enter in. We are to put the flesh-hooks of determination and discipline into the sacrifice and maintain it there. It must be yielded, yes, as a living sacrifice, a living sacrifice.

Holily

Brought yieldingly and livingly, yes – and brought as a holy sacrifice, holily to the Lord, laid on the altar. I came as a sinner just as I am, without one plea, but as a Christian I am to bring that life cleansed initially by the precious blood, but daily cleansed by that Word, that Holy Spirit, that purifying hope and all the means of grace, to keep that holy life before Him in an attitude of surrender. We are to render our sacrifice as a living sacrifice, as a holy sacrifice, and, notice, as a pleasing sacrifice.

Pleasingly

It is to be yielded pleasingly to Him. That word 'pleasing sacrifice' is a reference back to the ascending offering that went up in the tabernacle as well as the temple, behind that first veil. So that whether people saw that ascending sacrifice or not, that incense was ever rising to heaven, a beautiful picture of the life of the Lord Jesus who was totally yielded to the will of His Father, both in His private and in His public life. When He stood on the banks of the Jordan and presented Himself for His messianic ministry, identifying Himself with His redemptive work, you remember how heaven opened and God said from heaven, 'This is my beloved Son in whom I am well pleased.'

Looking back over that private life the word was, 'I am well pleased.' Jesus was the ascending offering, whether hidden or open, in His private and public life. Can you bring that life of yours tonight and say, 'Lord, here's my life, I bring it with yieldedness, I bring it as a living sacrifice, I bring it as a pleasing sacrifice'?

So many people are wonderful saints at Keswick, but demons back at home. Is your private life as pleasing to Him as your public life? The ramifications of true surrender. Paul is not just building up words for emphasis. He says that the plea for a surrendered life is the revelation of God's mercies in Jesus Christ, the expectation of that love He's poured out on us. But the pattern of surrender is that my response should be brought as a sacrifice, yieldingly, as a living sacrifice, a holy sacrifice, a pleasing sacrifice.

God's purpose for a surrendered life

Somebody says, 'To what purpose, to what end?' It is right here in our text. God's purpose for a surrendered life is in verse 2. To me, it is one of the greatest challenges of a life of surrender that I can find anywhere in Scripture. The meaning of this verse is simply this: God's purpose in a surrendered life is first of all the transformation of character, and then, the regulation of conduct.

The transformation of character
The transformation of character is put negatively at first. 'Be not conformed to this world.' That word 'conformed' is an interesting one. It is used by botanists, it is used by naturalists.

I am reminded of the chameleons I saw when I was a child on a mission station. So many Christians in our contemporary Christian world today are Christian chameleons. They go to a prayer meeting and so they say their prayers. They are in a group of people who use filthy language, so they join in. They eat among a crowd of people who are drinking, so they drink; and they are conformed to this world.

The cry of so many is, 'Get with it, get with it!' I read here in the Bible 'Get out of it, get out of it!' Sure, we are to be in the world, but not of it. We are to be holy, harmless, undefiled, separate from sinners. We are to be distinctive. We are to be known as Christians who have a mark upon them. Or, to put it into J.B. Phillips' translation 'Don't let the world around you squeeze you into its own mould.'

Negatively, it's non-conformity to the world, but positively, it's true conformity to the Lord Jesus through the renewing of our minds, as we are having done to us at Keswick as the Word of God is opened and expounded and applied by the Holy Spirit. There is a transfiguration taking place; the transformation of character.

But you know, that cannot happen and will not happen, until we are yielded, until our lives are brought yieldingly, livingly, holily, and, most importantly, pleasingly to Him. And as we are pliable on the altar of God's acceptance, He shapes us, remakes us, transforms us, transfigures us, into the likeness of the Lord Jesus Christ. God is far more concerned with what you are, than with what you do, and if what you are doesn't satisfy His holy demands, then what you do is virtually worthless.

The regulation of conduct

And so it moves right on from the transfiguration of character, to the regulation of conduct, 'That you may prove, that you may demonstrate, what is that good, acceptable, and perfect will of God.' Now that's not a trichotomy in the will of God. No, no. It's the one will of God, but it is described in this way purposely, because I believe there is a very real lesson to learn. It is the good will of God. God intends this to be profitable for us. It's not irksome, it's the good will of God.

I'll never forget preaching in our church in New York one

Sunday morning, on a theme very similar to this, and God moved in tremendous power, and there was a great response amongst young people. One young lady came forward and quietly sat at the front weeping. When I had a moment, I sat down alongside of her, and I said to her, 'Can I help you?' She said, 'I hope you can.' She said, 'I want to go all the way with Jesus, I want to serve Him for all the rest of my life, but I have a deep deep fear.'

And she looked up and she said something that stunned me, and yet thrilled me. Stunned me, because I hadn't heard it put quite that way, but thrilled me, because of her candour. She said, 'I'm just afraid that God's going to take a mean advantage of me.' And I took her to this very text, 'That you may prove what is that good will of God.' You see, God will not withhold any good thing from them that walk uprightly.

Pleasurable

But it's not only the good will of God, it's the pleasing will of God. There is joy in serving Jesus. There is fun in the Christian life. God intends us to enjoy Him, and to enjoy His service. That, I believe, is what the Lord Jesus meant when He said to those disciples who were far more interested in sandwiches than they were in souls – He said 'My meat – that which satisfies and sustains Me – is to do the will of Him who sent me, and to finish His work.'

Supremely of course it comes right to the heart of what I said at the beginning; it's the purposeful will of God. We shall never come to wholeness, to our true humanity, redeemed in Christ, into all that God intends for us down here in our condition, and one day in heaven in our conservation; we won't fulfil His purpose in His good and acceptable and perfect will – until we are totally yielded.

Peter dropped at the feet of Jesus and said, 'Lord, depart from me, for I am a sinful man, Oh Lord. I am not worthy of You, but I own Your lordship because I have seen You work. You deserve all I have. Everything I have is Yours.'

Jesus accepted him and said, 'I will make you a fisher of men.'

Paul takes up that same theme and says: that's how you answer the lordship of Christ. That's how you answer the wonderful redemptive love of God in Christ. And so he says, 'I call you alongside. I plead with you. I beseech you.' God's plea for a surrendered life.

What is your answer to His love? God's pattern for a surrendered life: you must come with that yieldingness, that yieldingness which is a once-for-all act that you maintain with an attitude of surrender to the end of your days. Come with that livingness of being one with Jesus in resurrection life, with death to self, life in Christ, with a holiness of life, word thought and deed. Like an ascending offering, pleasing Him, knowing very well as you surrender your life that a transformation is going to take place in your character, by the renewing of your mind, from centre to circumference. Less like the world, more like the Saviour, your life will be regulated in God's will, God's good and acceptable and perfect will.

A BLESSING IN DISGUISE

by Dr Roy Clements

John 16:7

'Tis better to have loved and lost, than never to have lost at all.' No, that's not quite the way Tennyson wrote it, is it? It's actually a parody by a satirist called Samuel Butler. But do you think that could ever be true? Do you think losing someone we loved could ever seriously be regarded as preferable to not losing them? It's hard to believe that isn't it?

And yet did you know that Jesus insisted that it was true, at least as far as He was concerned?

Open your Bible to John 16:7, and I think you will see what I mean. As Jesus speaks these words, He's on the threshold of arrest and execution. He's walking with His disciples to the Garden of Gethsemane, a familiar stroll which He is taking for the very last time, and He knows it.

The more He speaks of His departure, the more morbid and melancholy His disciples become. The discourse has more and more taken on the nature of a monologue, until Jesus Himself confesses to finding their gloomy silence depressing (verses 5–6).

His opportunity to speak to them is almost at an end. There is more He would like to say, but their faces betray their inability to cope with it just at the moment. So Jesus must bring His long farewell to a conclusion.

But before He does so, He tries to get them to look on the bright side of what is about to happen. 'You must realise,' He said, 'that losing Me isn't the disaster you think it is. If only you understood a little more, you would realise it's better to have loved Me and lost Me, than never to have lost Me at all.'

Look at verse 7. A counsellor, in the Greek, is usually someone who is called in to assist you when you are in trouble with the law. It could be a defence lawyer, a defence witness, or just a personal friend who came along to give you moral support in court.

But of course, in these chapters Jesus is using this word 'Counsellor', as a title for the Holy Spirit. He makes that very plain in chapter 14:16–17. 'I will ask the Father, and he will give you another Counsellor . . . the Spirit of truth.' 'There is no real need for despair at my departure,' He said, for I am going to send to you a personal companion to support you and encourage you – a Counsellor. Such a gift is He, that, with the benefit of hind-sight, you will be able to say when you look back on these events, "It was better to have loved Jesus and lost Him, because He sent the Spirit to us."'

Do you really feel that?

Well, I want us just to look at three vital areas of the Holy Spirit's work, so that we can get some perspective on just why it is so advantageous to us to live on this side of Pentecost.

The Spirit's distinctive work in the world

His work is a work of conviction. Verse 8: 'It's to your good,' He says, 'I am going away, for when the Counsellor comes, He will convict the world of guilt in regard to sin, righteousness and judgement.'

Why is it that a man who has lived in careless indifference to God for years is suddenly arrested by a sense of sin, the fear of death maybe, and a need of personal salvation?

Jesus tells us it is the work of the Holy Spirit. It is He who convicts the world of sin, righteousness and judgement. That word 'convict' describes what a lawyer does to a hostile witness. He's not just a defence lawyer, He's public prosecutor too, this Holy Spirit, this Counsellor. He convicts the world of guilt. Of course He's always done that. But if you look carefully at Jesus' words, you will see that with this new release of the Spirit that results from Jesus' departure, a radical change in the nature of that convicting work of the Spirit takes place.

There's a new focus now for the definition of sin that the Spirit applies – verse 9, '. . . Of sin' – because people break the Ten Commandments? No, 'because they do not believe in Me,' says Jesus. From now on, it's the rejection of Jesus which ultimately condemns the world. Contempt for God's law can be forgiven, but contempt for His Son – that can't. It is the Holy Spirit's work to expose to men and women the moral rebellion that hides behind the mask of their unbelief in Jesus. He convicts them of sin – sin defined as unbelief in Christ.

Again, there's a new certainty about the vindication of goodness in this conviction – verse 10: '. . . In regard to righteousness' – because God's standards are eternal? No, more than that, 'because I am going to the Father.'

There can be no doubt any longer. The kind of life-style that lasts is the life-style of the risen Lord, and it is the Holy Spirit's work to convince men and women that there is something absolute, something inescapable about the moral claim which that risen Lord makes upon them.

Thirdly, there is something else – there is a new urgency

about the imminence of the end of the world in this Holy Spirit's conviction (verse 11). '. . . In regard to judgement' – because sometime in the future God is going to call all men to account? No, 'because the prince of this world now stands condemned.'

It is the perfect tense. We are no longer talking about some far-off Day of the Lord, we are talking about something that has happened. With the exaltation of Christ, the Kingdom of God has arrived. So judgement is no longer a distant threat but an imminent crisis, in which each of us must take sides, either with this victorious Jesus who is risen and ascended, or with His defeated enemy, the Devil. 'And,' says Jesus, 'it's the Holy Spirit's work to inject that imperative call to decision into human hearts.'

In every way this convicting work of the Holy Spirit is enhanced and rendered more compelling by the departure of Christ. Before He went, vast multitudes of the human race successfully ignored God's claim upon their lives. But on the day of Pentecost alone, 3,000 men were, we read, cut to the heart by the apostles' words. The influence of Jesus today is a million times greater than it was 2,000 years ago during His own lifetime. And why? Because the Holy Spirit, the Counsellor, is convincing the world of its guilt.

There's immense encouragement here for us in our witness and our service and our preaching, too. When you read a passage like this you realise just how powerful preaching can be, or any kind of Christian witness, because the conscience of thousands of people are always on your side – this Counsellor is at work confirming the authority and significance of Jesus in people's hearts.

So there is nobody who can walk out of a place where God's Word is proclaimed without having felt the impress of that inner voice. Maybe some of you here this week have been conscious that God has been speaking in some way, but you have been worried – 'Maybe it's just my religious upbringing, or the emotional impact of the preacher's eloquence.'

May God forbid that I should be encouraging someone to be gullible and naive. But there's another explanation – that inward pressure could be the voice of the Holy Spirit challenging us. If that is so, we should be grateful, for even if we had Jesus Himself in His physical presence before our eyes, He could not communicate so great a persuasion of the truth as that invisible presence of the Counsellor in your heart this evening. That's the first reason it's to our advantage that Jesus goes away, because this Counsellor, with His unique work in the world, comes to our aid.

His distinctive work in the apostles

I suspect the words of John 16:12-15 are among the most important and potentially dangerous words that Jesus ever spoke. They are important, because they explain to us why Jesus never wrote anything during His lifetime. He never seems to have bothered to pick up a pen, in spite of the fact that He clearly believed His authority was greater than the prophets.

Have you ever wondered why that was so? Was it because He anticipated the ministry of the Holy Spirit in His disciples? It would be the distinctive task of the Spirit to perpetuate the special revelation of what Jesus had wrought, and to guide the disciples into all the truth.

Therein of course, lies a danger. Many have seized upon these words as proof of a continuing gift of inspiration in the church, as a consequence of which we may expect new revelations of the Holy Spirit even today.

But I have to tell you that I do not think that that interpretation can be substantiated by the rest of the New

Testament, or even by this passage. There is a distinction to be observed between the application of such words to Christian believers generally, and their special application to those to whom Jesus was immediately speaking when He spoke them in the first place.

Jesus is here using the plural 'you' in this farewell discourse. He is not speaking directly to us, He is speaking directly to the Eleven – we only overhear. Of course, the vast majority of what He was saying to them in the first century is, generally speaking, true for us in the twentieth century. But we must not conclude that Jesus intends to say everything to us in exactly the same way as He said it to them. There are some things that are not transferable.

The revelation of new truths after His death is something which is limited to the apostles. He promises that the Holy Spirit will give a total revelation to the apostles themselves. And that is certainly the way they understood it, because, as Michael Baughen has been saying of 2 Timothy, you don't find the apostle at the end of 1 Timothy telling the church to look for more inspired apostles and prophets who can continue to expound new truths for the church's edification. You find them instead warning in the severest terms against false prophets, and urging the church to faithfully transmit that body of the gospel truth, that they, the apostles, once and for all, had delivered to the saints.

The first century apostles were distinct, you see, from other Christians. That is why Paul can talk about the church being built upon them. In that sense, what He is saying here is something we have to be very careful to apply in a unique way, to Jesus' apostles – they were promised a special revelation of the Spirit. It would help them to understand Jesus and His significance, in a way they had not done before.

Of course, there is an application of His words for us. It is through the Holy Spirit that the New Testament is illumined to us. If we did not have the Holy Spirit, then just like the Jews of the Old Testament, there would be a veil over our eyes and we would not understand the Bible.

In that more limited sense, Jesus' words are applicable to all of us. It has to be stressed; illumination is different from inspiration. Inspiration is a gift for understanding new truths, and that is what Jesus is specifically promising here in chapter 16. Illumination is a gift of understanding old truths. That's why Peter's sermons go into the Bible, and mine have to come out of it.

But this is the second great advantage which the Holy Spirit brings us – He brings us the New Testament, He brings us an understanding of Jesus and His work through the apostles, that we could not have had if we had been there with Jesus, in the days of His flesh. It is only since His departure that this revelation, this instruction far beyond anything we could have enjoyed, had Jesus not departed, has come to us.

Sometimes, we do find people have an altogether too romantic idea of the blessing of actually being there. Sometimes, they take trips to Palestine, and they wax eloquent about the nostalgia of standing where Jesus stood, and imagining themselves hearing the Sermon on the Mount from His lips, and so on. 'Oh,' they say in all simplicity, 'if only we had been there on the hillside, what an impact, wouldn't it have been marvellous.' No doubt it would. But not more than the privilege of sitting with the text of that Sermon on the Mount from the pen of the Spirit of the inspired author, in front of our very eyes.

Jesus is telling us in these verses that the possession of the New Testament is a greater blessing than to have actually heard the voice of incarnate Deity with our physical ears. That's something, isn't it? The gift of the Spirit of Jesus, in inspiring the apostles, is a gift of vast magnitude. 'It's to your advantage I'm going away.'

And there is a third blessing.

The distinctive work of the Holy Spirit in the individual Christian

It's a work of consolation.

Look at verse 16 of this chapter. 'In a little while you will see me no more, and then after a little while, you will see me.' One of the things which C.S. Lewis, in his book *A Grief Observed*, observed about the experience of losing his wife was that it did not help very much when people told him about the value of memories.

Of course he was right. Sentimental memories make it hard, not easier, to come to terms with loss. Jesus, in these chapters, understands that memories are important. He has instituted a feast just before, with the words, 'Do this in remembrance of me.' But He understands that memories are not enough. We need the personal presence of Christ in our lives. And that is precisely what He is promising.

If you look back to chapter 14, you will see an interesting word in verse 16 – 'I will ask the Father, and He will give you another Counsellor.' Who was the previous Counsellor? Why, of course, it was Jesus. He had been their Counsellor up till then; their friend, their supporter, their advocate, their helper. But now He was going to the Father. Someone else, another, would continue to exercise that same role towards them.

At least, I say 'someone else'; but it may be too strong a phrase. Do you notice the subtle way that Jesus seems to pass from the third person into the first, when He is talking about this Counsellor?

> The world . . . neither sees him, nor knows him. But
> you know him, for he lives with you and will be in you.
> I will not leave you as orphans; I will come to you.
> (John 14:17)

You get the same kind of ambiguity in chapter 16:16.

What is He talking about? The resurrection appearances? The second coming? Maybe; but almost certainly, He is primarily talking about the Spirit. He portrays Him here really as Himself, in another form, another Counsellor, 'Like Me, but different'.

Such is the mystery of the Trinity, that in giving us the Spirit, Jesus is giving us Himself. Can you think of a blessing greater than that? To have the Spirit of Jesus in you?

If I'm honest, I have to say that it is possible to make too much of the Holy Spirit. Sometimes, you come across groups that seem to think that the work of the Holy Spirit is completely confined to the church, which of course it isn't.

The Holy Spirit has a greater distinctive work in the world, which world God so loved that He gave His only Son; He sent that Spirit out to convict the world of sin and judgement and righteousness. That's why Christians have to be involved in the world in that sense, following the Spirit where He goes.

Sometimes you find groups where you hear a lot about the Holy Spirit, but not a lot about the Bible. Again, there is no coincidence in that, for these Christians tend to think that the Holy Spirit renders the Bible almost unnecessary, and again, you see it is a misunderstanding, because it is the Holy Spirit who has inspired the New Testament. Those apostles are mediating to us Spirit-given truth, and that is our access to the truth through the Scripture.

It's not as if we have a private hot-line to heaven. Again,

sometimes you come across groups where you hear a lot about the Holy Spirit, but strangely little about Jesus. But these verses make it quite clear that's a misunderstanding, for Jesus is really the Holy Spirit in a different form, and the Holy Spirit is Jesus in a different form.

Jesus Himself said, 'The Holy Spirit is the most modest and self-effacing person of the Trinity. He will bring glory to Me, by making what is Mine known to you. He won't speak about Himself, He'll only talk about Me.'

It is possible to make too much of the Holy Spirit. But I have to tell you, it's far more lethal an error to make too little of the Holy Spirit.

Show me a church centred round the sacraments, for instance, with no real awareness of the Holy Spirit dwelling within a believer; or show me a church obsessed with theology and good doctrine, and no real awareness of the Holy Spirit dwelling within a believer, and I'll show you a dead church. It's the Holy Spirit who makes the church alive – it's He who turns Jesus from being a mere hero of the past, a mere memory commemorated in a book and in our rituals, into our living contemporary.

According to Jesus, if it is a choice between standing amongst the crowd who saw Him in first century Palestine, and standing amongst us here in the congregation of the twentieth century church, a wise man would choose to stand with us.

The question we have to ask ourselves this evening, is whether the Spirit has brought Jesus alive into our experience in that way. There is absolutely no need for nostalgia where Christ is concerned. He is the one person in the world whom it is better to have loved and lost. The truth is, we have not really lost Him at all.

THE REVELATION REVOLUTION

by Bishop Michael Baughen

Ephesians 1:17–23

You and I are in a love relationship with the Lord. We are part of the bride betrothed to the bridegroom. The Holy Spirit has brought us to new life, brought us into the family and made us in love with Christ. But a love relationship takes time and it's something that needs to go on growing and developing and deepening, with all its joy and sometimes its pain, with all its wonder, with all its new discovery.

How many Christians do you know, who've been stuck since conversion, who've not really grown year by year in the graces and gifts of the Spirit and the joy of the Lord, and all that it means to grow towards the measure of the stature of the fullness of Christ? I'm afraid it's true of many Christians.

Now there are many reasons why that may be so. It may be indiscipline, it may be carelessness, but one of the reasons I believe is right under our nose, in the New Testament. When you look at Paul's prayers in the New Testament, and this is one of them in Ephesians 1, he prays ninety-nine percent of the time for the spiritual growth of Christians. And I honestly believe that this is something that the church and we Christians, have often failed to see.

I believe part of the problem is that we haven't prayed in terms of growth. Put a group of Christians together, and they will pray for someone's bunion, or their particular need, or something wrong at home, or that they will have a safe journey. But these things are not the major concern. The Christian is concerned to know most of all, how is he growing in Christ; how much is he knowing of the grace of the Spirit; how much is he growing towards the measure of the stature of the fullness of Christ?

This is the deep concern of the New Testament and a deep prayer concern of Paul's. He is praying here for a spirit, and of course he is referring to the work of the Holy Spirit. A Spirit of revelation in the knowledge of Him 'having the eyes of your hearts enlightened'. It is a concern which, I believe, we need to lay hold of together, for it is only the Spirit of God who can show us more of the Lord, who can draw out the truth that He has given us once and for all in the New Testament, and can teach us more of those truths, and dig further into them, and understand more of the love of the Lord. It is only the Spirit of God who searches the hidden things of God, 1 Corinthians 2, who alone comprehends the thoughts of God; for He reveals to babes what is hidden to the wise and understanding.

Thus I would want to call this address tonight, 'The Revelation Revolution'. The more the Spirit of God shows us God and the things of God, the more it should have a revolutionary effect in our lives for Him.

Now there are three things which the Spirit reveals in this particular passage.

The hope to which God has called us

The first is in verse 18. It is the revelation of the hope to which God has called us. The Holy Spirit deepens our understanding and our assurance of that sure and certain hope. Don't be intimidated by the world's jibes at us, because it is helpless and hopeless in the face of death. What can it say? There's no reunion to look forward to; no life ahead; no hope. As far as most of the world is concerned, all the character and training and personality and gifts of a person who has died have ended in death. That is what so much of the world believes, and it is pathetic.

The world does not like to speak about it, because it is worried about it. And in the face of that, we have a glorious hope through Christ, to go home and be with Him, to be absent from the body and present with the Lord, to the place prepared and the Lord coming to receive us. Isn't it marvellous?

Paul quotes that little phrase from 1 Corinthians 2, 'What no eye has seen, nor ear heard, nor the heart of man conceived, what God has prepared for those who love Him.'

Somebody wasn't thinking when they composed the funeral service in the New Alternative Service Book in the Church of England, because that's where they stopped the quote. Amazing!

Listen. 'What no eye has seen, nor ear heard, nor the heart of man conceived, what God has prepared for those who love Him' – can you end it? – 'God has revealed to us by His Spirit.' God has done that already. It's wonderful. What is impossible to find out humanly, God has revealed to us in these glorious insights about the glory ahead, which we now have in the New Testament.

But there is more. The Spirit, as you know, is the downpayment, the first-fruits, the first taste of heaven, and it is often in worship that He opens heaven up to us.

Now worship is often called the gate of heaven. That's a wonderful description of what worship ought to be. Do you know that wonderful phrase in Hebrews 12:22, 'You have come' – not 'will come' – 'You have come to Mount Zion, to the city of the living God, the heavenly Jerusalem, to innumerable angels in festal gathering, to the assembly of the firstborn, who are enrolled in heaven, to a judge who is God of all, to the Spirit of just men made perfect and to Jesus'?

You have come.

Every man and woman in Christ in this tent is already locked into heaven, because we're citizens of heaven. And when we worship together, we are caught up with the great assembly. That is why, in the middle of the communion service, for many of us, there is that expression, 'So with angels and archangels, and with all the company of heaven'.

Hebrews 12 goes on, 'Let us therefore be grateful for a kingdom that cannot be shaken, and let us offer to God acceptable worship with reverence and awe.' Is your worship like that in your church? It is the reality of the living God in the midst, and people meaning business with God, that is the key to worship. And that can be true in all sorts of churches.

Some of you may have been to Switzerland, and you'll know that if you go up the Jungfrau Railway from Interlaken, on the last stage you go on the line that took eighteen years to carve through the solid rock of the Eiger. You look out through the window, and there is the top of the Jungfrau with the snow glistening in the sun and the blue sky behind it, and everybody stands at the window, and says, 'Oh, that's terrific'. Then boom! – the train goes into the tunnel.

For ten minutes it grinds up in the darkness, and it stops. They've carved a station out of the rock, with windows out on to the valley. Everybody pours out of the train and rushes to the window, and says, 'Oh, it's even better, it's marvellous.' Then back in the train, boom, boom, boom, ten minutes up through the tunnel again.

Another station! Out they get again, this time right up in the glacier, snow all around them, the sun sparkling. Superlatives are not sufficient. Then, back into the tunnel, and up you go again, and at last you're there. Walking in the snow for yourself, there at the destination, and it's incredible.

That for me is a little bit like what worship's supposed to be. When we meet together, it's like being released out of the train for a bit. Here we are released together, and there's a glimpse of heaven, of God meeting with His people and us with Him. That's terrific! And bit by bit, when we come to worship, we keep having a foretaste of heaven until – we're there!

The Holy Spirit is there to give us the foretaste of heaven to open up what it's going to be like. It is God's hope to which God has called us, and which God wants us to know more and more. And He does so, as this text tells us, in response to prayer for the Spirit of God to reveal, and, of course, the hope is supremely that we shall be with Him and see Him as He is, and worship Him for ever.

The riches of His glorious inheritance

Secondly, the Spirit of God reveals to us 'the riches of His glorious inheritance in the saints.' It's almost impossible to expound this, because the riches are so great and inexhaustible. How do you cope with it in exposition? But that's part of the point – there is so much to learn of God's provision for His people, that it is inexhaustible. And even if every day God showed you something fresh from His Word, from His truth, you still would not exhaust all that He wanted to teach you.

When I was first ordained, I panicked. I thought to myself, goodness, I might be forty years in the ministry, I wonder how many sermons I might preach – but as I grew older, I realised that if I lived to three hundred and fifty, I could never exhaust the riches of the Word of God and all that He wants to show us.

This is the incredible thing about the Word of God. It goes on yielding and yielding. There's no other book in the world like that. And this is why; it is the Spirit's book and the Spirit is its interpreter. And you know as well as I do, that when you first come to Christ, one of the results is that it begins to open up. No one told me it was going to do that and I was so surprised. I suddenly found myself sitting up into the night for hours on end, reading the Scriptures. Though I'd flogged at them before, now it was like food and drink, I couldn't get enough of it. That's what the Spirit does, He opens up the riches of the Word of God.

Have you grown tired of the Word? I hope not. Do you think the Word is a bit jaded? If you've grown tired it's you, not the Word.

Of course, this is only part of it. It's also the way in which He shows us the inheritance of being one of His children. Here in the tent, on the top of a mountain, in a double-decker bus, sitting at our office desk, anywhere, we can always just slip straight into the Father's presence and bring Him our needs and talk to Him and share things with Him. This is part of the wonderful inheritance we have as the children of God. And how much of all that He wants to do for us and for our churches is held back because we do not draw on the riches of our inheritance, by prayer.

'My God will supply all your needs' – that is a great part of our inheritance. He guides us, He blesses us, He moves with us in evangelistic conviction, as we've just been hearing; He brings growth, He brings fruit, He brings gifts for service. We can hold on to the fact that 'All things work together for good to them that love God'. I have no time to expound. I would be here for weeks to expound the riches of the inheritance, but the Spirit of God is there to open it up to us all the time. Supremely, the riches of our inheritance are that we are the Lord's. You are Christ's, and all that is Christ's is yours.

When I was at All Souls, we entered into a fairly large building project, which cost a lot of money – about £650,000. We started with about £20,000 in the bank. The only way to provide a place of meeting was to excavate under the church, and we actually went down thirteen feet, and dug out all the earth around the pillars into the earth. We worshipped in the meantime crowded into St Peter's, Vere Street. One Sunday evening half way through the project I was walking back on my own from St Peter's. It was the end of the day. I went into Cavendish Square, which was deserted. Suddenly I was grabbed with panic. Here we were halfway through, all the earth had been excavated, you couldn't put it back; and we hadn't got anything like the money – perhaps half. I thought, 'What on earth will happen if we don't succeed?'

It was one of those occasions when I almost physically felt His arms go round me. And the words just breathed through my mind, 'Well, Michael, if you do fail, I will be with you in the failure.' That was all I needed, and on I went through Cavendish Square. The hug of the Lord. Have you known that in a moment of testing or problem? It's wonderful to know the Lord in this way, isn't it? And it's part of the inheritance of being in Him, to know more and more of the love of God which surpasseth knowledge, but which, because it is limitless, the Holy Spirit can continually open out.

Those of you who are older, who've been Christians for many years, should know how, across the years, the Holy Spirit has opened up more and more and more of what it means to be part of the family of the Lord. Is that true?

The immeasurable greatness of His power

Finally, there is the third revelation: the immeasuabe greatness of His power in us who believe (verse 19). The Holy Spirit is the Spirit of power. He came in power and He empowers all in Christ to serve and be God's men and women in the world. Paul is so excited about the power of God in the believer that he simply can't throw enough words into this sentence. There are actually four different Greek words he uses about power – strength, energy, force, robustness. They're all cascading one over the other.

But *is* it Paul? No! We believe that Paul is inspired by the Holy Spirit. The Holy Spirit is excited about it. And Paul becomes excited about it, and you and I should be excited about it. God wants to show us more and more of the immeasurable greatness of His power in us – in *us* – who believe. Not out there; in us who believe.

It is God's power, not our power. It is therefore a supernatural power and it is immeasuably great. How's it expressed? Well, in many ways. In Acts 2, it's expressed particularly in *boldness*, in the languages of the world, communicating the gospel. In Acts 4:31, when they come back after having been in the battle already, and pray to God, sovereign God, they throw themselves on the Lord. What happens to them? They are given boldness by the Spirit.

In Acts 7, Stephen is being stoned to death, but he's full of the Spirit – and what is the evidence? His boldness with the truth. One of the gifts of the power of God in us, is exactly what Timothy was having to learn; that is, there's a gift not of timidity, but of boldness, to declare the faith even in opposition.

The power is expressed in *miracle*. A miracle is a concentration of God's power at a particular point for a particular need and always for His glory. A miracle may overrule circumstances. It may be in healing. It may be in deliverance from prison. As we pray, God's power intervenes. Not everyone has their circumstances overruled, nor is everybody healed, nor is everybody delivered from prison. But God does come into those circumstances, and thousands of similar circumstances in answer to prayer, with what we can only call a miracle.

He is a God of power. To demand it on every occasion for every sickness is not New Testament faith. But nonetheless, to restrict God so that He can't do things is ridiculous. God is the God of all power and might.

Then power is expressed in the New Testament in *endurance*. We've been thinking about that in 2 Timothy and 2 Corinthians 4:7. You and I have this treasure of the gospel in earthen vessels. Earthen vessels are breakable, throwaway, disposable, to show what? To show that the transcendent power belongs to God and not to us. If you and I were super-people then the power of God in us would not be evidenced.

God is able to move in the most fragile earthen vessel with His power. This is the triumph of God's power in His servants; we share the sufferings of the world, it's how we endure them that is the testimony to the world that we have the power of God. Or it's the power of God in inner strength, Paul's prayer to know Christ and the power of His resurrection. The inner strength, 'My power made perfect in weakness.' That marvellous statement of Paul!

But it's always His power, verse 20. It is the same power that was accomplished in Christ. Look at it – the power that raised Christ, that has set Christ above all powers and dominions, that has made Him head over all things for the church. It is the same power which the Spirit brings in the believer. There's no limit to this power. However weak we may be physically, we need never be weak spiritually, for the power of God is within us by His Spirit.

This then is what the Spirit wants to go on and on doing in us. He wants to show us more and more of the Lord, whom we love and to whom we belong, but at the same time, He wants to show us more and more of what it means to be engaged to the Lord. Thus He reveals more and more of the hope to which He has called us, all that lies ahead and the great bridal feast; that we might delight in the prospect ahead, foretasting it often before.

Let me ask you; do you want this? Do you want to have more and more of the foretaste of heaven? Then ask God that His Spirit might go on showing you. He wants to reveal more and more of the riches of His glorious inheritance, so that we may dig in the riches and draw on the riches and not nibble at them.

Do you want this? Then ask God that His Spirit will go on showing you more of the riches of your inheritance. He wants to reveal the immeasurable greatness of His power in us who believe, that we may draw more and more on that power; that we may serve and work and weep and rejoice and be salt and light to this world, and His hands and His feet, and His mouth, to the spiritual and physical needs of this desperately needy world.

Do you want that power? Then ask God that His Spirit will go on opening that power and renewing it within you.

All this is summed up as the Spirit shows us more and more of the Lord Himself – and this is the Spirit's greatest joy to do – and as a result, brings into your life and mine the revelation revolution. To the glory of God.

KESWICK 1985 TAPES

Here is a list of tape numbers for all the messages in this book. The numbers follow the sequence of the contents.

Bible readings:

Rev Eric Alexander: 931, 932, 933, 934
Bishop Michael Baughen: 961, 962, 963, 964

Addresses:

Rev Eric Alexander	930
Rev Donald Bridge	948
Rev Kenneth Prior	951
Mr Alan Nute	952
Rev Philip Hacking	953
Rev Michael Wilcock	954
Rev Eric Alexander	955
Rev Gordon Bridger	968
Rev David Jackman	969
Dr Stephen Olford	972
Dr Roy Clements	973
Bishop Michael Baughen	974

These tapes can be obtained, together with a full list of Keswick tapes, from:

The Keswick Convention Tape Library
13 Lismore Road
Eastbourne
East Sussex
BN21 3BA.

KESWICK 1986

The annual Keswick Convention takes place each July at the heart of England's beautiful Lake District. The two separate weeks of the Convention offer an unparalleled opportunity for listening to gifted Bible exposition, experiencing Christian fellowship with believers from all over the world, and enjoying something of the unspoilt grandeur of God's creation.

Each of the two weeks has a series of four morning Bible Readings, followed by other messages throughout the rest of the day. The programme in the second week is a little less intensive, and it is often referred to as 'Holiday Week'. There are also regular meetings throughout the fortnight for young people, and in the second week for children.

The dates for the 1986 Keswick Convention are 12–19 July and 19–26 July. The Bible Reading speakers for the two weeks are Rev Dick Lucas and Canon Keith Weston. Other speakers during the fortnight, subject to final confirmation, include Dr James Boice, Bishop Maurice Wood, Rev Jonathan Fletcher, Rev Derek Cleave and Rev Philip Hacking.

Further details may be obtained from:

The Keswick Convention Secretary
25 Camden Road
London
NW1 9LN